Legal Office Projects ^{2e}

Legal **Office Projects** ²ᵉ

Diane M. Gilmore, PLS

Nashville, Tennessee

THOMSON
SOUTH-WESTERN

Australia · Brazil · Canada · Mexico · Singapore · Spain · United Kingdom · United States

THOMSON

SOUTH-WESTERN

Legal Office Projects, 2E
Diane M. Gilmore

VP/Editorial Director
Jack W. Calhoun

VP/Editor-in-Chief
Karen Schmohe

Acquisitions Editor
Jane Phelan

Project Manager
Dr. Inell Bolls

Consulting Editor
Barbara Tietsort

Marketing Manager
Valerie A. Lauer

Production Project Manager
Colleen A. Farmer

Manufacturing Coordinator
Charlene Taylor

Marketing Coordinator
Kelley Gilreath

Production House
Interactive Composition
Corporation

Printer
Globus

Art Director
Linda Helcher

Internal Designer
Michael Stratton

Cover Designer
Michael Stratton

Front Cover Photo Credit
© Getty Images

For more information about
our products, contact us at:

Thomson Higher Education
5191 Natorp Boulevard
Mason, Ohio 45040
USA

Table of Contents

Welcome

Welcome

Delete Reply Reply All Forward Print

From: Reginald J. Davis and Associates
Subject: Welcome
Date: First Day on the Job
To: Legal Office Assistant

We are pleased with your decision to join the legal support staff of Reginald J. Davis and Associates, where you will be employed as a legal office assistant in a floater position. Founded by Reginald J. Davis 25 years ago, our firm provides client representation in a wide variety of areas, including litigation, general business, real estate, criminal defense, estate planning, and dissolution of marriage actions.

There are currently two partners and two associates in our office. As a legal office assistant floater, you will be called upon to perform work for all of the attorneys in the firm as needed. In addition to the attorneys, the firm employs various legal and office support personnel. The organizational chart on page **x** lists the names of our employees and the positions they hold in the office. As you can see, your position is included among those of the legal support staff (See Figure A — Organizational Chart).

Our goal is to provide the best legal services available to our clients. As an employee of Reginald J. Davis and Associates, you are now a member of this highly respected legal team. Again, welcome to the firm and good luck on your new job!

Job Description

REGINALD J. DAVIS AND ASSOCIATES

Job Description

Delete   Reply   Reply All   Forward   Print

From: Reginald J. Davis and Associates
Subject: Welcome
Date: First Day on the Job
To: Legal Office Assistant

Job Title: Legal Office Assistant

Job Qualifications:
- Must be able to key 35 wpm and have basic knowledge of *Microsoft Word* software.
- Must have a basic knowledge of English grammar, punctuation, capitalization, and number style.
- Must be able to read and follow written and oral directions.
- Must be able to digitally transcribe from computer.

Job Duties:
- Prepare memos, correspondence, and legal documents for the attorneys as needed; This will be done by transcribing from dictation, keying text from rough draft copy, or preparing documents from forms on the computer;
- Prepare the initial paperwork required for new client files;
- Maintain all files in a neat, orderly condition and computer folders in an organized fashion;
- Request checks for disbursement to clients or other vendors for the firm, and other duties included in the accounting process of the firm as needed;
- Assist the bookkeeping department and the attorney in the preparation and timely completion of bills to be sent to clients when needed;
- Maintain the office calendar when required;
- Research the Internet for information relevant to a case the firm is handling;
- Any other duties that may be assigned to you.

A Firm Organizational Chart

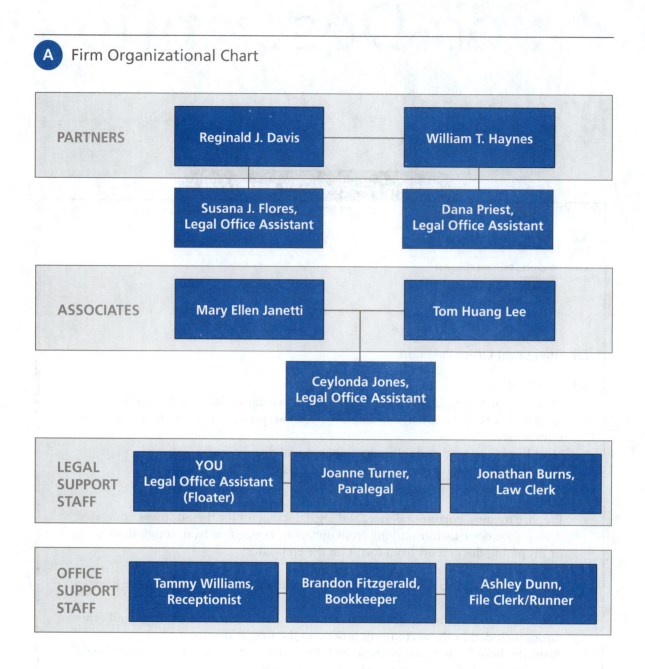

PARTNERS

Reginald J. Davis

William T. Haynes

Susana J. Flores,
Legal Office Assistant

Dana Priest,
Legal Office Assistant

ASSOCIATES

Mary Ellen Janetti

Tom Huang Lee

Ceylonda Jones,
Legal Office Assistant

**LEGAL
SUPPORT
STAFF**

YOU
Legal Office Assistant
(Floater)

Joanne Turner,
Paralegal

Jonathan Burns,
Law Clerk

**OFFICE
SUPPORT
STAFF**

Tammy Williams,
Receptionist

Brandon Fitzgerald,
Bookkeeper

Ashley Dunn,
File Clerk/Runner

Getting Started

The legal office assistant who can competently and professionally produce documents pertaining to every activity practiced by the firm is a vital member of any successful law firm. As a legal office assistant, you will be expected to perform traditional clerical duties in the specialized environment of a law firm. *Legal Office Projects* provides you with a real-life, hands-on opportunity to participate in the document preparation activities of a typical law office and perform effectively in the legal office environment.

Upon completion of this text, you will be able to:
- Demonstrate basic composition skills by creating letters and memos.
- Practice decision-making skills in preparing and formatting court papers, legal instruments, and other documents.
- Use the Office Procedures Manual to locate specific information required for completing your work.
- Key documents from draft or dictation in the correct format.
- Use the Transcription CD and computer software to prepare documents using advanced features of *MS Word*.

Organization of Text and Tasks

The instructions for the 12 projects and 4 case studies in this text represent work performed in a variety of legal fields during a typical day in a legal office. They are provided in an easy-to-understand scenario presented in a conversational format by the attorney for whom you are working. Some scenarios contain special software tips to improve your document-processing skills. Each project also contains a Legal Focus that will reinforce your knowledge of the law regarding a particular legal topic. The tasks presented in each project give you practice in doing the work required and applying the document preparation skills learned in your course of study. Carefully read the message from each attorney and perform the tasks presented in each project.

Decision-making and composition skills are important. You will be required to make formatting decisions regarding the documents you produce, and compose correspondence to various individuals in the simulation. The final work product must be acceptable by legal office standards. Your work must be complete, accurate, neat, and properly formatted according to the specification set forth in the Office Procedures Manual located on the CD. Proofread and correct your work before submitting it to your instructor. When you complete the documents in each project, submit them to your instructor for evaluation. Your instructor will provide you with feedback about the quality of your work as the course progresses.

File Management

Knowing how to organize, locate, and save the files you will create and use will make you more productive while using this text. You will open forms or create documents on a blank screen, print the document, and save it using a new filename.

If your classroom does not use a document management program, you will need to create a file management structure so that your work is saved in an organized fashion. This file management structure should be set up using another CD or diskette.

Begin by planning the organization of files on your storage device. One way to keep your files organized in this course is to organize work by projects. When you begin a new project, create a central folder for all of the documents in that project by name or project number (e.g., RUIZ or PROJECT-4). Next, create a subfolder for all of the work done in that project by task number and filename (e.g., T4-5 RUIZ.LTR). Another way to organize files is to delineate them by file type by placing all work from the project tasks into folders according to the type of document created (e.g., CORRESPONDENCE, PLEADINGS etc.).

Creating Folders. Once you have devised a strategy for managing your files in this course, you will create folders and organize files within them as you progress thorough each project. To create a folder, do the following:

- Select **File, New,** then **Folder** from the drop-down menu on the top tool bar, or move your mouse pointer and click on the folder button positioned on the tool bar. A boxed icon and the highlighted words, New Folder, will appear on the screen. Key in the desired name of the folder and press Enter. You now have a new folder where you can store new and existing files.
- Next create a subfolder by task number and filename for all of the tasks to be completed within that project.
- Repeat this procedure each time you begin a new project in this course
- Before saving the next document you create, locate the folder where you want to store the file. Then save the document in the selected folder.

Moving and Copying Data into Folders. From time to time, your instructor may direct you to move certain files into folders, or you may want to place a file located on the Transcription CD into a folder on your storage device.

To move a file using the "click-and-drag" method, do the following:
- Point to the file you want to move; *right click* to highlight and drag the file to the new folder. The file now appears in the new location. It is no longer in its original location on the Transcription CD.
- To Copy a file, point to the file you want to copy; *left click* to highlight it. Press the CTRL key and left click. Drag the file to the new folder; when the folder is highlighted, release the CTRL key.

To move a file using the cut and paste feature, do the following:

- Open Windows Explorer, and highlight the file or folder you wish to move or copy.
- Select Cut from the drop-down Edit menu at the top of the Windows Explorer screen if you are moving the file or folder. Select Copy from the drop-down Edit menu if you are copying the file or folder.
- Click once to highlight the destination folder where you want to store the file or folder you are moving or copying.
- Select Paste from the drop-down Edit menu. The file or folder will be moved or copied to the selected folder.

You can also move and copy multiple files by selecting a group of files and performing the same functions as above. To select files that are listed to-gether in a folder, click on the first file in the list, hold down the SHIFT key, click the last file in the list, and then release the SHIFT key. To select files that are not listed together, click on one file, hold down the CTRL key, key on the other files, and release the CTRL key. Then copy or move the files as indicated above.

Supplies

In this course you will prepare documents on the computer from rough draft, dictation, or by using forms retrieved from the Transcription CD, using the advanced features of *MS Word*. The Transcription CD contains the office letterhead, memo format, various professional legal forms, and other relevant data pertaining to the project tasks. Instructions for the various tasks will direct you to retrieve documents or locate dictation to be transcribed from the CD. Insert the CD into the CD-ROM drive, locate the designated file or dictation, and follow the outlined task instructions to complete the document. You will save your work to your storage device.

Bracketed text in the Transcription CD form files indicates points where information needs to be inserted. Because it is easy to overlook this text, use *MS Word's* search feature to locate all brackets in the file. When you have made the necessary additions or changes to the form document, you will be directed to resave the document using a different filename, to keep the original form document intact.

Use the dictation files on the Transcription CD to transcribe documents as indicated in the task section of the instructions. Insert the Transcription CD into the CD-ROM drive and locate the attorney's dictation pertaining to a particular task. Complete the document as dictated by the attorney, using the format illustrated in the Office Procedures Manual.

Use plain paper for pleadings, court papers, and other documents created in this text. Although there are specific instructions in the tasks to create envelopes for correspondence, your instructor may prefer that you either obtain envelopes and prepare them to accompany correspondence, or simply print the envelope on plain paper.

Office Procedures Manual

You will frequently be referred to the Office Procedures Manual, located on the CD, for additional assistance. The Office Procedures Manual contains standard reference information such as two-letter state abbreviations as well as examples of documents prepared at Reginald J. Davis and Associates. You should consult the Office Procedures Manual before beginning a task, especially if you need particular information to complete a task, and refer to it to confirm specific formatting requirements for each type of document.

Internet Activities

Where applicable, you will be called upon to locate sites and perform research using the Internet to obtain information needed for certain tasks. These Internet activities are designed to challenge you to research information on the Web and apply that information appropriately to complete a particular task.

Critical Thinking Activities

Each project contains a detailed Critical Thinking activity designed to reinforce a particular legal topic and encourage discussion. The questions presented in the Critical Thinking activities may be assigned by your instructor as homework or can be completed as a group to generate further class discussion of the topic.

Legal Focus

Each project has an informative Legal Focus that discusses real-life legal issues commonly encountered in a law firm. These informational snippets highlight terminology and situations that may arise in particular legal fields and help broaden your knowledge of a particular legal topic.

Participating in the real-life routine of this course will make practicing the fundamentals of legal document production meaningful and interesting. After completing the projects outlined in this text you will be able to locate documents and other information appropriate to a particular situation, identify the information necessary to complete the documents, and prepare the final documents accurately and efficiently. Practicing your newly acquired document production skills in this setting will better prepare you for a rewarding career in today's legal field.

TRANSCRIPTION PROCEDURES

1. Prepare Your Workstation

Your workstation should include the following minimum specifications:

- A computer with *Microsoft Word 98SE, ME, 2000,* or *XP,* 233 MHz processor; 64 MB RAM; 100 MB free space on the hard disk; and a 16-bit sound card.
- A printer or access to a printer if you are sharing printers in the classroom.
- A ⅛" mini-plug headset connected to your computer to use with the Transcription CD.
- Transcription CD loaded into your computer.

2. Prepare Your Computer

Special note regarding use of Transcription CD: Depending on the transcription method you are using, you may use a foot pedal, mouse, or keystrokes to start, stop, rewind, and fast-forward your dictation. Your instructor will assist you in determining which method you will use with this course. When you hear the instruction "Release your foot pedal," you will use your chosen method to stop the dictation.

The Transcription CD offers you a choice of either *Express Scribe* or *Windows Media Player 10.0* playback software for use while transcribing the dictated files. Instructions for accessing the files for each software application appear below.

To install the playback application: Select either *Express Scribe* (preferred) or *Windows Media Player.* Click on the button to install the preferred software. The program will be installed on the computer, and an icon will be placed on the computer desktop. Once the software is installed, the student needs to select it from the main menu each time the CD is used.

Directions for using *Express Scribe* (foot pedal or keystroke control method):

a. Plug your headset/foot pedal into the computer using the manufacturer's recommended settings.

b. Insert the Transcription CD and select "Use Express Scribe" from the main menu.

c. Select the designated task and *Word* template you wish to open, and click the "Launch" button. The program will automatically open *Word* and *Express Scribe.*

d. If you are using hot keys (function keys) to operate the dictation playback, here is a listing of some of the hot keys you will want to use to control the dictation:

F4 Stops the dictation
F9 Plays the dictation

F7 Rewinds the dictation

F8 Fast-forwards the dictation

Important Note to *Express Scribe* Users: The program automatically saves a copy of the audio file in its directory with an 8.3 filename. To avoid confusion, delete these files from the *Express Scribe's* directory upon completion of the lesson.

Directions for using *Windows Media Player 10.0* (mouse control method):

a. Plug your headset into the computer using the manufacturer's recommended settings.

b. Insert the Transcription CD and select "Use Windows Media Player" on the main menu.

c. Select the designated task and *Word* template you wish to open, and click the "Launch" button.

d. *Word* will launch, and the *Media Player* console will appear on top of it. Use your mouse to increase and decrease the volume, start and stop, fast-forward to the end, or rewind to the beginning.

FORMS LIST FOR TRANSCRIPTION CD

File Name	Form Title	Project/Task Number
AFFIDAVIT	Affidavit	3-2
ART-OF-INC	Articles of Incorporation	11-1
BILL-FORM	Monthly Billing Statement Form	2-1; 5-5; 11-6; CS-6; CS-11; CS-23
BILL-OF-SALE	Bill of Sale	7-4
BYLAWS	Corporation Bylaws	11-4
C-BROCHURE	Criminal Law Brochure	9-7
CHECKREQ	Check Request	1-3; 2-6; 4-8; 6-3; 8-5; CS-5
CLIENT-INFO	New Client Information Sheet	4-1
CLIENT-INFO-CRIM	New Client Information Sheet – Criminal Matter	9-1
COI-FORM	Conflict of Interest form	4-2; 9-2
COI-MEMO	Conflict of Interest memo	4-2; 9-2
DEMAND-FOR-DISCOVERY	Demand for Discovery	9-5
DIRECTIONS-CLERK	Directions to the Clerk	12-3
DOM-FINAL-JUDGMENT	Diss. of Marriage – Final Judgment	CS-21
DOM-FINANCIAL-AFF	Diss. of Marriage – Financial Affidavit	CS-15
DOM-INTERROGS	Diss. of Marriage – Interrogatories	CS-7
DOM-MSA-DRAFT	Diss. of Marriage – Marital Settlement Agreement – Draft	CS-19
DOM-NOTICE-FILING	Diss. of Marriage – Notice of Hearing	CS-17
DOM-REQ-PROD	Diss. of Marriage – Request for Production	CS-8
DPOA-HEALTH	Durable Power of Attorney for Health Care	5-4
EXPERT-LETTER	Expert witness letter	6-4
FINANCIAL-POA	Financial Power of Attorney	5-3
INTERROG-FORM	Interrogatories	8-1
JOINT-STIP	Joint Stipulation	10-1
LETTERHEAD	Letterhead	1-3; 2-2; 3-4; 4-5; 4-6; 5-6; 7-1; 8-6; 11-2; 11-7; CS-1; CS-16; CS-22
LIVING-WILL	Living will	5-2
MEDICAL-AUTH	Medical authorization form	4-4
MEMO	Memorandum	1-1; 1-5; 1-7; 2-4; 6-5
NOLIEN-AFF	No-Lien Affidavit	7-5

(continued)

File Name	Form Title	Project/Task Number
NOT-GUILTY-PLEA	Written Plea of Not Guilty	9-4
NOTICE-APPERANCE	Notice of Appearance	9-3
NOTICE-DEP	Notice of Taking Deposition	8-3
NOTICE-HEARING	Notice of Hearing	CS-10; CS-13; CS-18
NOTICE-OF-APPEAL	Notice of Appeal	12-1
ORG-MINUTES	Organizational Minutes	11-3
PARTIAL-BRIEF	Partial appellate brief	12-4
PETTY-CASH-VOUCHERS	Petty cash vouchers	2-5
POLICE-LTR	Letter to police department	4-7
POWER-OF-ATTY	Power of Attorney	3-3
QQDEED	Quit Claim Deed	CS-20
REPORTER-DESIG	Designation of Reporter	12-2
REPRESENT-AGR	Representation Agreement	4-3
RESPONSES	Responses to breakfast meeting	1-4
SELF-PROV-AFF	Self-proving affidavit	5-1
SETTLEMENT-STMT	Settlement statement	2-3
STOCK-CERT	Stock certificate	11-5
SUBP-DT	Subpoena Duces Tecum	8-4
SUMMONS	Summons	6-2; CS-4
TRAVEL-EXPENSES	Travel Expense Report	1-6
TRAVEL-REQUEST	Travel Request Form	1-2
TRIAL-SUBPDT	Subpoena for Trial Duces Tecum	10-5
UCCJEA-AFF	UCCJEA Affidavit	CS-3
WARRDEED	Warranty Deed	7-3

General Office Procedures

From Attorney Davis

Please take care of the travel arrangements and paperwork for a seminar that Tom Lee and I are attending on the 17th, and prepare the expense reports when we return the following day. Let me know what you find regarding the travel and car rental costs from the Internet. Keep in mind that we would like a nonstop flight during the day. I would also like a master list of those attending this month's Downtown Lawyers Association meeting. Locate some local caterers who could provide a breakfast refreshment break at the meeting for about 35 people for under $500, and give me a list of those establishments and the services they provide. Finally, please prepare the documents regarding our firm's new conflict of interest policy.

tasks

 1-1 Research Internet and prepare memo to attorney

1-2 Prepare travel requests

1-3 Prepare check request and seminar letter

 1-4 Create table of breakfast meeting responses

1-5 Research Internet and prepare memo to attorney

 1-6 Prepare seminar expense reports

1-7 Prepare conflict of interest policy, memo, and form

PROJECT 1

PHOTO: © Ryan McVay/Photodisc/Getty Images

Research Internet and Prepare Memo to Attorney

1. Refer to the Office Procedures Manual on the Transcription CD to review the firm's travel policy and instructions about obtaining approval for law firm trips.
2. Research the Internet for the best rates for air travel and car rental accommodations, noting the flying preferences requested by Attorney Davis. Conduct a general Internet search, or use specific airline or car rental company sites to compare rates. Choose the best option for air travel and car rental rates.
3. From the Transcription CD, open the **MEMO** file. Prepare a memo to Attorney Davis regarding your findings, indicating which web sites were searched and your reasoning for selecting the indicated travel arrangements. Upon completion, save the document as **T1-1 DAVIS-MEMO1** and print one copy of the memo.

Prepare Travel Requests

Open the **TRAVEL-REQUEST** file. Complete a travel request form for each attorney, using the information on the seminar form in Figure 1-2. Upon completion, print one copy of the completed forms and save the completed documents as **T1-2 TRAVELREQ-RJD** and **T1-2 TRAVELREQ-THL,** respectively.

L E G A L   F O C U S

Conflict of Interest
A conflict of interest is a situation in which someone, such as a lawyer or public official, has opposing interests that might make it difficult to perform his/her legal and ethical duties to a particular client. For example, a conflict of interest would arise if a lawyer simultaneously represented two clients who were adversaries in a case. Similarly, it would be a conflict of interest for an attorney to testify as a witness in a case in which he/she is representing one of the parties. Engaging in a case in which a conflict of interest exists may expose an attorney to disciplinary action, reversal of proceedings, and malpractice claims. As these consequences can easily be averted by performing a simple conflict of interest check, it is crucial for the legal office staff to be well versed in all aspects of uncovering, examining, and verifying potential conflicts.

 Seminar Form

---

LEGAL SEMINARS INCORPORATED
"USING MEDICAL RECORDS IN LITIGATION"
Chicago, Illinois, February 17, 20XX

REGISTRATION INFORMATION:

Payment Policy: Registration fees are payable in advance. Attendees may pay by check, Visa, MasterCard, or American Express.

Group Discounts: Groups of 2–9 from the same organization, attending at the same location, are entitled to a 10 percent discount. For groups of 10 or more please contact us at (800) 555-0123 for further discount information.

CLE Credit: This course is approved for 7 hours of CLE credit, 2 hours of which will apply to legal ethics and 5 hours to law practice management.

Our Guarantee: If this seminar does not meet your expectations, please call (800) 555-0150 for a full tuition refund.

Tuition and Time: Tuition for this seminar is $199 per person (includes manual), prepaid. The seminar runs from 8:30 a.m. to 4:30 p.m.

REGISTRATION FORM:

Seminar Name: "Using Medical Records in Litigation"
        February 17, 20XX, Hilton West Hotel, Chicago, Illinois, $199
        Speaker: John Van Zant, Esq., University of Illinois Law School

Firm Name: _____
Street: _____
City: _____
State: _____ Zip: _____

Detach and Mail to:

LEGAL SEMINARS INCORPORATED
P.O. Box 1899
Chicago, IL 60601-4833

Bus. Phone: _____
Bus Fax: _____

Method of Payment:
☐ Check ☐ Visa
☐ MasterCard ☐ American Exp.

Card No. _____
Expires: _____

By Fax: Complete this form including
        credit card information and
        fax to: (800) 555-0142

Prepare Check Request and Seminar Letter

1. Open the file **CHECKREQ**. Using the information on the seminar form, complete the check request. Determine whether the firm qualifies for a discount, and if so, calculate the reduced amount of the check. When finished, save the completed document as **T1-3 SEMINAR CHECK** and print one copy of the request.
2. Open the **LETTERHEAD** file. Using the information from Attorney Davis and the seminar form, prepare a letter with an envelope to the seminar sponsor and enclose the check and registration form. Upon completion, save the document as **T1-3 SEMINAR LETTER** and print one copy of the letter and envelope.

Create Table of Breakfast Meeting Responses

1. Open the **RESPONSES** file. Review the list of responses to the breakfast meeting. Use the information from the list of responses to create a table that contains columns for the name of each guest who responded, the firm at which that individual works, the number of people attending from that firm, the entrance fee paid, and if not paid, a column to indicate the nonpayment.
2. Use landscape paper orientation. Begin by keying the heading, "Downtown Lawyers Association Idea Exchange Meeting," and the date, in boldface; and the title, "Attendance List," in all caps, boldface, and underlined. Then key the table underneath the title. Be sure to create separate columns for the first and last name of each person attending to sort by last name later. Format the table so that all the information fits in one cell. Apply other formatting features (such as bold or centering) to make the table look attractive on the page.
3. Sort the table alphabetically by last name of the guest responding.
4. Upon completion, save the document as **T1-4 RESPONSE LIST** and print one copy.

PAPER ORIENTATION—To change paper orientation, click File, Page Setup, and select Landscape in the Margins tab portion of the window.

SORT—To sort items in a table, place the cursor in the table and click Table, Sort. Select the column to sort by last name column, and then click OK.

Research Internet and Prepare Memo to Attorney

1. Research the Internet for at least three establishments in your city (restaurant or catering company) for menu choices and prices offered for the breakfast meeting break. For each vendor, calculate the price per person indicated on the web site times the number of people attending the breakfast meeting. Be careful not to exceed the $500 budget allotted for the refreshments.
2. Open the **MEMO** file. Prepare a memo to Attorney Davis outlining your findings about catering choices for the breakfast meeting. Indicate the names of some establishments that could cater the event, the menu for the breakfast break offered by each establishment, and the price charged per person. When finished, save the completed document as **T1-5 MEETING-MEMO** and print one copy.

Prepare Seminar Expense Reports

You will prepare an expense report for each attorney's attendance at the CLE seminar for reimbursement. You have the figures obtained in Task T1-1 for the flight and car rental expense. Each attorney has written down additional expenses for you to incorporate into the forms.

1. Refer to the Office Procedures Manual on the Transcription CD to review the firm's policy and instructions about obtaining reimbursement for law firm trips.
2. Open the **TRAVEL-EXPENSES** file. Prepare a travel expense form for each attorney, using the information given earlier by Attorney Davis and additional expenses from each attorney provided in Figure 1-6. Format the document accordingly to be sure that when adding information, the entire document stays on the same page. Upon completion, save the document as **T1-6 SEMINAR EXP-RJD and T1-6 SEMINAR EXP-THL**, respectively, and print one copy of the completed form.

 Expenses

RJD's Expenses

Dinner on 2/16: see below
Breakfast on 2/17: $15.76
Lunch on 2/17: $19.18

Gas for rental car: $29.43
*Please put entire cost of rental car on my
expense report, as we both shared the car."

Entertainment: "Tom and I took
Councilman Jones and his wife out for
dinner on 2/16: $215 – share cost
between Tom and me."

THL's Expenses

Dinner on 2/16: see below
Breakfast on 2/17: $12.90
Lunch on 2/17: $18.86

1-7 Prepare Conflict of Interest Policy, Memo, and Form

Attorney Davis is instituting a new conflict of interest policy for the firm. He has dictated the general policy to be added to the firm's Office Procedures Manual. He also dictated a memo that will be circulated around the office when a conflict of interest question comes up, as well as changes to a Conflict of Interest form created by Attorney Huang. You will transcribe the dictation and make the changes on Attorney Huang's form.

1. Open the dictation file **T1-7 CONF-OF-INT POLICY** and key the document as dictated by Attorney Davis. Upon completion, save as **T1-7 COI-POLICY** and print one copy of the document.
2. Open the **MEMO** form. Then open the dictation file **T1-7 CONF-OF-INT MEMO**. Transcribe the memo dictated by Attorney Davis. Upon completion, save the document as **T1-7 COI-MEMO** and print one copy of the memo.
3. Create the Conflict of Interest form as indicated on the attorney's draft in Figure 1-7. Upon completion, save the document as **T1-7 COI-FORM** and print one copy of the completed form.

1-7   **Form with handwritten changes by attorney**

Conflict of Interest Search Form   *First two lines: Center, all caps*
(Privileged and Confidential)   *and bold*

Italics   Potential Client: *Double-space between*
Name: *first line italics and*
Other names and/or nicknames: *"Name"*
Address:
Spouse's name:
Spouse's other names:
Opposing parties' names:
Associated persons or entities: *<* *Put here in italics: "Determine which area is*
                                involved and enter the names, etc. of the other
Bold all the If a litigation matter, indicate: *persons involved."*
"if..." lines. Plaintiff:
Defendant: *Change the word "indicate:" in every line to*
Insurer: *"who is/are the"*
Expert witnesses:

If a divorce matter, indicate:
Client: *Adjust margins, etc. to*
Spouse: *keep text on one page.*
Children (with ages)   *RJD*

If a corporate, business, or real estate matter, indicate:
Owner/spouse:
Buyer:
Partner:
Seller:
Officers/Directors/Shareholders:

If an estate matter, indicate:
Testator/testatrix:
Spouse/children/heirs:
Trustee:

If a criminal matter, indicate:
Accused:
Victim:
Co-Defendant:

Critical Thinking

1. Indicate some follow-up tasks concerning the legal education seminar that you can perform prior to the seminar date.

2. Indicate ways that the breakfast meeting attendance list you created stays current and that no names are duplicated in the days preceding the event.

Legal Office Accounting

From Attorney Janetti

I have dictated an interim bill and cover letter for our client, Michael Blumberg. He paid a $500 retainer, so be sure to give him credit on the bill. We have also settled the case of our client, Patsy Reynolds, against Crystal Lumber Company for $125,000. There is a memo on your desk outlining the costs in the case. Please prepare the settlement statement and calculate a net figure for the client. Then prepare a memo for me indicating the amount of our fee collected and the net amount due to the client. Also, remind me to call the client to come in to sign the settlement statement. Finally, please reconcile our petty cash fund and request a check from the bookkeeper to reimburse it.

tasks

2-1	Calculate and prepare invoice
2-2	Prepare letter to client
2-3	Prepare settlement statement
2-4	Prepare memo to attorney
2-5	Prepare Petty Cash Transaction Record
2-6	Calculate and request petty cash reimbursement

Calculate and Prepare Invoice

1. Refer to the Office Procedures Manual and study the format, billing rates, and other information for preparing the firm's billing invoices to clients.
2. Open the **BILL-FORM** file. Key the current date in the appropriate place on the document.
3. Open the dictation file **T2-1 BLUM-BILL**. Listen to the dictation and key the information into the billing form as dictated by Attorney Janetti. Credit the client for the funds advanced, and calculate the final amount due from the client. When finished, save the document as **T2-1 BLUMBERG-BILL** and print one copy of the document.

Prepare Letter to Client

Open the **LETTERHEAD** file used in Project 1. Open the dictation file **T2-2 BLUM-LETTER,** transcribe the dictation, and key the letter as dictated by Attorney Janetti. Prepare an envelope for the letter. When finished, save the document as **T2-2 BLUMBERG-LTR** and print one copy of the letter.

Prepare Settlement Statement

A settlement statement sets forth a detailed accounting of the money spent and received on behalf of a client. In the matter of <u>Patsy Reynolds versus Crystal Lumber Company</u>, Circuit Court Case No. 2X-11894, the defendant's insurance company has settled our client's claim for $125,000. Law Clerk Brandon Fitzgerald left a memo on your desk outlining the costs advanced in the case. The firm's standard fee in a contingency fee case is 33-1/3 percent of the gross proceeds.

Open the **SETTLEMENT-STMT** file. Using the information contained in the memo from Brandon Fitzgerald to you in Figure 2-3, prepare the settlement statement by inserting the name of the case as well as the settlement amount, attorney's fees, and costs into the form. Calculate the net amount due to the firm and to the client. When finished, save the document as **T2-3 REYNOLDS-STMT** and print one copy of the settlement statement.

2-3 Reginald J. Davis and Associates

Reginald J. Davis and Associates

MEMORANDUM

TO: (Name of student)

FROM: Brandon Fitzgerald

DATE: March 18, 20XX

SUBJECT: Patsy Reynolds v. Crystal Lumber Company

Pursuant to Mary Ellen Janetti's request, below is a list of unpaid medical expenses and other costs pertaining to the above case:

Unpaid medical expenses:

A-1 Ambulance Company, $266.75
The Chiropractic Academy, $845.00
County Pathology, $234.00
Southside Physical Therapy, $742.50
Best Orthotics Company, $1,338.00

Costs Advanced:

Filing fee, $300.00
Service of process fee for Crystal Lumber: $55.00
Service of process fee for Richard Harrison, $30.00
Service of process fee for Anita Dearborn, $30.00
Downtown Court Reporters: Deposition of Richard Harrison, $220.00
Justice Court Reporters: Deposition of Anita Dearborn, $185.00
Deposition Fee for Dr. Jackson: $400.00

If you need anything further, please let me know.

Prepare Memo to Attorney

Open the **MEMO** file. Compose a memo to Attorney Janetti, attaching the settlement statement and indicating the amount due to the firm for its fee and the net amount due to the client. Remind Attorney Janetti to contact the client to come in and sign the settlement statement. When finished, save the document as **T2-4 MEJ-MEMO1** and print one copy of the memo.

Prepare Petty Cash Transaction Record

1. Open the **PETTY-CASH-VOUCHERS** file and review the list of petty cash vouchers used by the firm.
2. Use the information from the vouchers to create a table listing the expenditures by category that later can be recorded in the firm's accounting program. Create the table containing columns with the following headings: Date, Paid To, Balance, Paid By, Office Supplies, Postage, Meals, Taxi, Tolls, and Misc. Then create a row above the headings to key the title, "Petty Cash Transaction Record," and the dates the vouchers cover. Begin with an entry titled "Beginning Balance" for the beginning balance of $200 on 2/14/XX. Then list the expenditures in chronological order.

LEGAL FOCUS

Legal Office Accounting
Most law firms track time and expenses with special legal billing software that enables the attorney or staff to enter time spent, expenses incurred, and payments received on a particular matter. Automated billing ensures efficiency and accuracy of the firm's billable time. As a legal office assistant, you will often be required to prepare a billing statement or reconcile a client's funds with the firm. Whether preparing a client's invoice from billing software or manually, it is vital to be familiar with the firm's time and billing procedures as well as basic account principles. Be sure to include all billable time from all sources, including other attorneys or timekeepers in the office. Also, be sure to enter all expenses incurred on behalf of the client. Carefully examine the client's cost account to verify all payments, costs, and other transactions involving the client's case and apply those transactions to the client's billing invoice or settlement statement.

3. After you have entered all the vouchers into the table, add a row called "Total Expenses," reflecting the total amount of the vouchers. Then add a row called "Ending Balance" and calculate all the expenditures subtracted from the beginning balance. This figure is the amount needed to replenish the petty cash fund. Apply other formatting features such as margin adjustments, bold, centering, and column adjustments to make the table look attractive on the page. When finished, save the document as **T2-5 PETTYCASH-REPORT** and print one copy.

Calculate and Request Petty Cash Reimbursement

Open **T2-5 PETTYCASH-REPORT** from the prior task. Open the file **CHECKREQ** used in Project 1. Using the information on the form and the Petty Cash Transaction Record, prepare a check request for reimbursement of the petty cash fund to replenish it back to $200. When finished, save the document as **T2-6 PETTYCASH-REQ** and print one copy of the check request.

Critical Thinking

Do you believe a firm can ethically collect an expense, even a large one, that was advanced but inadvertently omitted from the settlement statement that was already signed and approved by the client? Indicate ways a firm can alleviate a problem like this from occurring in the future.

Legal Document Preparation

GENERAL
POWER OF ATTORNEY

From Attorney Lee

Please prepare a non-compete agreement I have dictated for my nephew, Funio Hyashi, a local disc jockey. Please also edit and finalize the changes I have dictated to an affidavit for our client, Timothy Craig. Then prepare a power of attorney form for our client, Maria Lupita, appointing her two sons, Manuel and Juan Carlos Lupita, as her designated attorneys-in-fact, to manage her affairs. I have dictated changes to the form along with a letter to her about the document. Finally, add a client contact form to our firm's web site. I have made a drawing of the Web page design. Please create a draft of the form for us to work with when making revisions with our Webmaster.

tasks

3-1	Prepare Non-Compete Agreement
3-2	Edit and finalize an affidavit
3-3	Prepare Power of Attorney
3-4	Prepare letter to client
3-5	Prepare an online client information form

Prepare Non-Compete Agreement

1. Refer to the Office Procedures Manual on the Transcription CD to review the format, signature clauses, acknowledgements, and other information used in preparing legal documents for the firm.
2. Open dictation file **T3-1 NON-COMPETE** dictated by Attorney Lee and transcribe the contract agreement. Upon completion, save the document as **T3-1 HYASHI-AGMT** and print one copy of it.

Edit and Finalize Affidavit

1. Refer to the Office Procedures Manual to review the format of affidavits used by the firm.
2. Open the **AFFIDAVIT** file. Correct any typographic and punctuation errors you find in the document.
3. With the affidavit still open on your screen, open the dictation file **T3-2 AFFIDAVIT CHANGES**. Key the changes to the affidavit dictated by Attorney Lee. Upon completion, save the document as **T3-2 BOYD-AFFIDAVIT** and print one copy of it.

Prepare Power of Attorney

Open the **POWER-OF-ATTY** file. With the affidavit still open on your screen, open the dictation file **T3-3 POWER-OF-ATTY CHANGES**. Transcribe the dictation and key the changes to the document dictated by Attorney Lee. Upon completion, save the document as **T3-3 LUPITA-POA** print one copy of it.

Prepare Letter to Client

Open the **LETTERHEAD** file and open the dictation file **T3-4 LUPITA**. Transcribe the letter dictated by Attorney Lee and key an envelope to the client. Upon completion, save the document as **T3-4 LUPITA-LTR** and print one copy of the letter and envelope.

Prepare an Online Client Information Form

1. Refer to Attorney Lee's drawing in Figure 3-5 to review his idea for an online client information form. Create a template of the online form and save it as **T3-5 ONLINE-FORM**.

    a Use creative features such as different font choices, sizes, and colors to format the title and subtitle of the form. Insert an appropriate clip art image where indicated.

    b Create a borderless table in the template for the data entry lines of the form.

    c Display the Forms toolbar to create the form fields requested by Attorney Lee, including text, drop-down, and check box form fields.

    d Use color and texture from the Drawing toolbar to place a rectangle around the data entry area to apply a parchment texture to the form, as requested by Attorney Lee.

2. After designing the online form, protect the form so that users can enter data only in the designated form fields. Upon completion, resave the document for later use and print one copy of the contact form draft.

SOFTWARE tip

DRAWING TOOLBAR—To view the Drawing toolbar, click View, Toolbars, Drawing.

SOFTWARE tip

ANIMATED TEXT—To animate text, select the text to be animated. Right-click the selected text, click Font on the shortcut menu, and click Text Effects when the Font dialog box displays. Click one of the animation choices in the Animations list and then click OK.

3-5   Handwritten Drawing of Client Information Page

REGINALD L. DAVIS   (center)
AND ASSOCIATES   (center)

add legal clip art on both sides of name

Attorneys and Counselors at Law   (center)
Free Case Evaluation!
Complete form and press "submit"

Please complete the following form telling us about your case. We will review your submission and promptly contact you with our determination of whether we can help you obtain relief under the laws of this state. There is absolutely no charge or cost to you for this service!

If you prefer, you may contact us at 1-800-555-0100 for a free case evaluation by one of our experienced attorneys.

Client Information Sheet

Today's Date:
Name: _____
Address: _____
City: _____
State: _____
Zip Code: _____
Home Phone: _____
Work Phone: _____
When may we contact you? (choice of days or evenings)
Nature of Problem: (check boxes for: Litigation, Personal Injury, Criminal, Family Law, or Other)
Description of Problem: _____

This box parchment style

SUBMIT button   CLEAR FIELDS button
WE'LL PROTECT YOUR RIGHTS!   (center and make flashing)

Internet Activity

Locate one or more web sites that provide information about different power of attorney documents and when each type is used. Search under obvious words, such as "power of attorney" or "legal definitions," or you can search web sites of specific law firms in your area that specialize in the preparation of these types of documents. Review the list of sites and links for the information you are seeking and research those sites accordingly. List your results, including the Internet sites from which you obtained your information.

L E G A L   F O C U S

Law Firm Web Sites

Many law firms maintain web sites on the Internet to market their services to clients worldwide and to enable both existing clients and potential clients to communicate with them. Providing a client information form on a law firm's web site encourages visitor interaction and also allows attorneys to accept online inquiries, capturing important information about these potential clients. An attractive, user-friendly form can be created in minutes and can be modified easily as situations change, saving the firm the expense of printing and maintaining an inventory of forms that may become outdated quickly. Providing client information forms on the firm's web site not only provides such accessibility but also saves the firm time and money by expediting communication with potential clients and eliminating the need for a paper inventory.

Critical Thinking

Besides a non-compete agreement, what other types of agreements would an attorney in a law firm prepare? Create a list of the agreements and the circumstances surrounding each type.

Opening File Procedures

From Attorney Haynes

Prepare a New Client Information Sheet and other related paperwork for our client, Carmella Ruiz, regarding her car accident last month. I have placed the notes of our discussion on your desk; they contain all of the information you will need. Then transcribe the letters I have dictated to Ms. Ruiz and the adverse party letter to the defendant. Also, send a letter to the Fort Lauderdale Police Department for the police report and include a check for its fee. Finally, please complete a conflict of interest check from the policy and memo prepared earlier by Mr. Davis.

PHOTO: © Ryan McVay/Photodisc/Getty Images

tasks

4-1 Prepare New File Information Sheet

4-2 Prepare conflict of interest paperwork

4-3 Prepare Agreement for Representation

4-4 Prepare medical authorization

4-5 Prepare letter to client

4-6 Prepare adverse party letter

4-7 Prepare police department letter

4-8 Prepare check request

Prepare New File Information Sheet

Open the **CLIENT-INFO** file. Use the information contained in Attorney Haynes's handwritten notes in Figure 4-1 to prepare the New File Information Sheet. Upon completion, save the document as **T4-1 RUIZ-INFO** and print.

Prepare Conflict of Interest Paperwork

1. Open the **COI-FORM** file. Use the information contained in Attorney Haynes's handwritten notes (Figure 4-1) to insert the required information at the top and in the Litigation section of the form. Upon completion, print one copy of the agreement and save the document as **T4-2 RUIZ-COIFORM**.
2. Open the file **COI-MEMO**. Use the information contained in Attorney Haynes's handwritten notes (Figure 4-1). Compose a memo to Carmella Ruiz; include all required information.
3. Upon completion, attach the agreement; save the document as **T4-2 RUIZ-COIMEMO** and print one copy of the memo.

Prepare Agreement for Representation

Open the **REPRESENT-AGR** file. Use the information contained in Attorney Haynes's handwritten notes (Figure 4-1) to insert the required information in Section 1 and at the bottom of the agreement. Upon completion, save the document as **T4-3 RUIZ-AGR** and print one copy of it.

4-1   Handwritten Notes

Client: Carmella J. Ruiz (husb. is Carlos Ruiz) Her nicknames are
Carmelita and Candy. Main name was Carmella Hernandez
627 South Water Street
Sunrise, Florida 33322-3289
(954) 555-0124 (H)   (954) 555-0162 (W)
SSN: 555-66-0148   DOB: 1/4/54

Auto acc. – client was driving west on Church Street, turned north on
Sandy Shore Lane. Was struck by car that ran stop sign from the opposite
direction. Vehicle a total loss. Client taken by ambulance to Doctor's
Medical Center. Address: 5600 Independence Way, Fort Lauderdale-
33322-4955. Other party issued a citation.

Ambulance is County Ambulance Service, 1620 North Andrews Avenue
Fort Lauderdale, Florida 33130-3855.

Location of Accident: 2200 Sandy Shore Lane, Ft. Laud., at 9:00 p.m.
Date of Accident: 3/25/XX

Client works at Dreamtime Shoes in Miami – has not returned to work
since the accident due to injuries (broken leg, pain in neck, shoulders, and
back).

Fee – Contingency   OTHER DRIVER:
                                     Cindy Long
                                     13511 Kitt Drive
                                     Sunrise, FL 33323-9117

Need to Do:
* Open new file.
* Get police report – Ft. Lauderdale P.D. – Def. cited for DUI
* Get medical bills and records from all providers.
* Get copy of citation and court information for other driver.
* Start insurance claim for lost wages, medicals, and auto—her insurance
is Safe Drivers, Inc., Miami, Florida.

Client Dr. is:
Samuel Bishop, M.D. (555-0164)
300 Professional Plaza, Boca Raton, FL 33433-6880

Prepare Medical Authorization

Open the **MEDICAL-AUTH** file and complete the form. Insert the name of the health-care provider and patient in the spaces provided. At the bottom of the form, insert the name of the client, her date of birth, and her Social Security number. Upon completion, save the document as **T4-4 RUIZ-AUTH** and print one copy of it.

Prepare Letter to Client

Open the **LETTERHEAD** file used in Project 1. Open the dictation file **T4-5 RUIZ LETTER** and transcribe it. Key the letter dictated by Attorney Haynes and key an envelope to the client. Upon completion, save the document as **T4-5 RUIZ-LTR** and print one copy of the letter and envelope.

Prepare Adverse Party Letter

Open the **LETTERHEAD** file and the dictation file **T4-6 LONG LETTER** to the defendant, Cindy Long. Transcribe the letter dictated by Attorney Haynes and key an envelope to the defendant. Upon completion, save the document as **T4-6 LONG-LTR** and print one copy of the letter and envelope.

Prepare Police Department Letter

Open the **POLICE-LTR** file. Compose a letter to the police chief requesting a copy of the police report in the Ruiz/Long incident. Upon completion, save the document as **T4-7 RUIZ-POLICE** and print one copy of it.

Prepare Check Request

Open the **CHECKREQ** file. Complete the check request for the fee
required by the Fort Lauderdale Police Department to obtain the police
report in this matter. Upon completion, save the document as **T4-8 RUIZ-
CHECK** and print one copy of it.

L E G A L   F O C U S

Patient Confidentiality and HIPAA
In order for the firm to obtain medical reports and other information from doctors, hos-
pitals, and other medical providers who treated a client as a patient, the client must sign
a medical authorization form, giving permission for medical records to be released to
the client's attorney. The Health Insurance Portability and Accountability Act, or HIPAA
(pronounced "hippa"), passed by Congress in 2003 mandates a uniform set of standards
to ensure the privacy of an individual's health-care information and to strictly limit unauthorized disclosures without the patient's express permission. To obtain copies of a
client's records, a law firm's medical authorization form must now be HIPAA-compliant.
In addition, most attorneys will typically ask a client to sign several original undated and
unaddressed medical authorization forms to keep on hand in the event additional
health-care providers are identified later in the case.

Critical Thinking

How would you organize the electronic folders needed on your computer for the new Ruiz matter? List the subfolders necessary to effectively contain the different types of information that will be stored and used in the Ruiz case. Indicate the structure of the directory you might create to organize these subfolders.

Estate Planning

From Attorney Davis

Please prepare the estate planning documents for our clients, Solomon and Harriet Greenberg. I have dictated wills for each of them. Then prepare a living will, financial durable power of attorney, and durable power of attorney for each of the Greenbergs using the forms on our computer. Finally, prepare a billing invoice for $2,500 for the preparation of the estate planning documents, along with a letter I have dictated to the clients.

tasks

5-1 Prepare Last Wills and Testaments

5-2 Prepare Living Wills

5-3 Prepare Financial Durable Power of Attorney

5-4 Prepare Durable Power of Attorney for Health Care

5-5 Prepare billing invoice

5-6 Prepare letter to clients

Prepare Last Wills and Testaments

1. Refer to the Office Procedures Manual to review the format and preparation requirements for preparing will documents for clients.
2. Open the dictation file **T5-1 WILLS**. Listen to Attorney Davis's dictation, and transcribe the Last Will and Testament for Mr. Greenberg in a new document window. At the end of the will, insert the self-proving affidavit that will follow the testator's signature mentioned in the dictation by Attorney Davis, as follows:
   a. Open the **SELF-PROV-AFF** form.
   b. Copy and paste the text of the self-proving affidavit to the end of Mr. Greenberg's will. Insert the client's information where required in the text. Upon completion, save the will as **T5-1 SGREENBERG-WILL** and print.
3. Now use the completed will document for Mr. Greenberg as the basic format for preparing the will for Mrs. Greenberg, changing the names of the parties and gender references where required. Upon completion, save Mrs. Greenberg's will as **T5-1 HGREENBERG-WILL** and print.

Prepare Living Wills

Open the **LIVING-WILL** form. Prepare separate living wills for Mr. and Mrs. Greenberg by inserting the correct information into the appropriate places in the document for each client. Upon completion, save the living wills as **T5-2 SGREENBERG-LIV** and **T5-2 HGREENBERG-LIV**, respectively, and print one copy of each.

Prepare Financial Durable Power of Attorney

The Greenbergs would like us to prepare a financial durable power of attorney, which is a form located on our computer. They both would like to appoint each other as their respective attorney, with Rachel as the successor Agent, where applicable in the form.

Open the **FINANCIAL-POA** form. Prepare a financial durable power of attorney for each client by inserting the correct information into the appropriate places in the document. Upon completion, save the documents as **T5-3 SGREENBERG-FPOA** and **T5-3 HGREENBERG-FPOA**, respectively, and print one copy of each.

Prepare Durable Power of Attorney for Health Care

The Greenbergs would like us to prepare a durable power of attorney for health care, which is a form located on our computer. They would like their respective lives prolonged except in the case of a coma or an irreversible unconscious state. In paragraph 2 of the document, there are three possible provisions concerning a client's life support preferences. Locate the paragraph that best conforms to our clients' preferences before deleting the other provisions in that numbered section. In addition, they both would like to appoint each other as their attorney with Rachel as the successor Agent, where applicable in the form.

1. Open the **DPOA-HEALTH** form. Prepare a durable power of attorney for health care for each client by inserting the correct information into the appropriate places in the document.
2. In paragraph 2 of the document, select the paragraph that best conforms to the wishes of the Greenbergs, and then delete the other provisions in the paragraph, along with the bolded instructions in the form. Upon completion, save the documents as **T5-4 SGREENBERG-HPOA** and **T5-4 HGREENBERG-HPOA**, respectively, and print one copy of each.

Prepare Billing Invoice

Open the **BILL-FORM** file. Complete the billing invoice for the clients, indicating the flat fee of $2,500 for the preparation of the estate planning documents. Upon completion, save the billing statement as **T5-5 GREENBERG-BILL** and print.

Prepare Letter to Clients

1. Open the **LETTERHEAD** file.
2. Open the dictation file **T5-6 GREEN-LETTER**. Listen to the dictation and transcribe the letter dictated by Attorney Davis. Key an envelope to the client. Upon completion, save the document as **T5-6 GREENBERG-LTR** and print one copy of the letter and envelope.

L E G A L   F O C U S

End-of-Life Issues

The law provides all Americans with the right to make their own decisions about the medical procedures they choose to have if death is imminent or they are rendered to be in a permanent vegetative state. A health-care power of attorney appoints someone to ensure that one's wishes regarding his or her health care are carried out. Such an agent can make such decisions from the moment a person becomes unable to do so, without having to wait for a court proceeding to move forward with important medical decisions. A living will, also called a health-care directive or advanced directive, outlines a person's preferences if death is imminent or if a person is rendered to be in a permanent vegetative state. Since doctors are required by law to save a patient's life by whatever means necessary, a living will serves as a legal means through which one's end-of-life wishes can be known.

Internet Activities

Using the Internet, research the different types of documents an attorney may use in preparing a client's estate planning portfolio and the purpose of each type of document.

Critical Thinking

What is the meaning and purpose of a self-proving affidavit when used in wills? Explain the advantages or disadvantages, if any, of the use of these affidavits in estate planning documents.

Preparation of Complaint and Summons

From Attorney Haynes

I am ready to prepare and file the Complaint and Summons in the Ruiz matter. You will use the New Client Information Sheet you prepared for Ms. Ruiz in Project 4 to obtain some of the information we will need for the documents. First I will dictate the Complaint. Prepare the document for my signature using our standard pleading format. Then prepare the Summons using our standard form. Next, obtain the checks we need to file the Complaint and serve the Summons. The fee to file the Complaint will be $300; Markowitz and Sams will serve the subpoena. Their information can be found in our Office Procedures Manual.

I have made handwritten changes to the text of a form engagement letter to expert witnesses that Mary Ellen Janetti would like to use in her litigation cases. She drafted the letter before she went on vacation, but she would like to see my changes right away. Please use Track Changes to incorporate my changes, and save them in a separate version of the document. Then prepare a memo to me letting me know when the changes are made and the name of the file so I can e-mail it to Mary Ellen for her to review the changes. Thanks.

PHOTO: © Photodisc Collection/Getty Images

tasks

6-1 Prepare Complaint

6-2 Prepare Summons

6-3 Prepare check requests

6-4 Edit expert witness engagement letter

6-5 Prepare memo to attorney

Prepare Complaint

Refer to the Office Procedures Manual for the format, style, and other information used when preparing the Complaint. From the Transcription CD, open the dictation file **T6-1 COMPLAINT**. Transcribe the document as dictated by Attorney Haynes. Upon completion, save the document as **T6-1 RUIZ-COMPLAINT** and print.

Prepare Summons

Open the file **SUMMONS**. Using the information contained in Attorney Haynes's dictation and the New Client Information Sheet previously prepared in Project 4, prepare the Summons by inserting the required information into the appropriate places in the document. Upon completion, save the document as **T6-2 RUIZ-SUMMONS** and print one copy of it.

L E G A L   F O C U S

The Ethics of E-mail

E-mail is fast, convenient, and a mainstream tool in a law firm's daily communication with clients and internal communications among attorneys and staff. However, this digital form of communication presents an opportunity for inadvertent discovery or disclosure of confidential information over the information superhighway.

In the attorney–client privilege, the lawyer owes a duty to the client to maintain the client's confidences. To minimize the risk of interception or unintentional disclosure of confidential messages sent electronically, many law firms have adopted sophisticated technology to protect the privacy of their Internet communications, including the use of high-level message encryption software programs and firewalls to protect against hackers. Law firms also routinely attach warnings and disclaimers to their outgoing messages and web sites to protect against a malpractice claim for accidental disclosures of sensitive information.

Although the American Bar Association has ruled that unencrypted information transmitted by an attorney to a client does not violate the Model Rules of Professional Responsibility, the bottom line is that with all forms of electronic transmissions, including e-mail, lawyers should take measures to reasonably secure confidential information so that both the firm and its clients can take advantage of the benefits the Internet can provide.

Prepare Check Requests

From the Transcription CD, open the file **CHECKREQ**. Use the information given to complete the $300 check request for the Clerk of the Court in the Ruiz matter, filling in the required information. Upon completion, save the document as **T6-3 CHECKREQ-CLERK** and print. Then open the file **CHECKREQ** from the Transcription CD again. Refer to the Office Procedures Manual to find the fee charged by Markowitz and Sams to serve the Summons on Cindy Long. Complete the check request for Markowitz and Sams for the amount required. Upon completion, save the document as **T6-3 CHECKREQ-MARK** and print.

Edit Expert Witness Engagement Letter

1. Open the file **EXPERT-LETTER** from the Transcription CD. Before making any changes to the form, resave the document with a new name, **T6-4 MEJ-CHANGES**.
2. Review the handwritten changes made to the expert engagement letter by Attorney Haynes. (Figure 6-4). Using the Track Changes feature of *Word*, make the changes requested by Attorney Haynes. Upon completion, print one copy of the letter with Track Changes enabled and save the completed document again as **T6-4 MEJ-CHANGES-TRACKED**. Next, print a final copy of the letter without the changes showing and save as **T6-4 MEJ-CHANGES**.

TRACK CHANGES—To track changes, double-click the TRK status indicator on the status bar. Use the Reviewing toolbar to display and review tracked changes.

Prepare Memo to Attorney

Open the file **MEMO** from the Transcription CD. Prepare a memo to Attorney Haynes, letting him know that the changes to the expert engagement letter are finished and the name of the file under which the document is saved on the computer. Upon completion, save the document as **T6-5 HAYNES-MEMO** and print.

6-4 Original Letter with Handwritten Changes

Mary Ellen Janetti, Esq.
Sample Engagement Letter for Expert Witness Services

Dear Mr. Expert:

letter confirms

This ~~document will confirm~~ that we have retained you to represent our client in connection with the following matter:

(list matter here)

~~Pursuant to our agreement and our various conversations~~, You will provide services to our

independent professional

law firm as an   expert witness. Payment to you for
the services you provide will not be dependent upon your findings or the outcome of any

arbitration,   *nor on*

legal action, mediation, negotiations, ~~or~~ the amount or terms of any settlement of the underlying legal cause, nor on any contractual arrangement between ~~you~~ and any other person or party.

our firm

initial

You have indicated that your engagement fee for services is Three Thousand Dollars ($3,000.00), which shall be paid at the time you sign this letter and return it to us. Billings for services performed or expenses incurred shall be charged against the engagement fee until such time as it is spent.

We will compensate you for services rendered as follows:

Fees. (bold, underlined)

1.   We will pay you the rate of $150.00 per hour for all tasks performed in this matter, including but not limited to analysis, calculations, conclusions, preparation of reports, and necessary travel time. For testimony at deposition or trial, we agree to pay

(continued)

6-4 Original Letter with Handwritten Changes

you at the rate of $200.00 per hour, to be billed in hourly increments. This rate for testimony shall apply to all times I am at trial, including breaks to check your office voice mail.

Exhibit Preparation. (bold, underlined)

2. We agree to reimburse you for time spent preparing graphics and exhibits for trial at the rate of $100.00 per hour, ~~even if you employ someone else to perform the services~~ if you outsource the services.

regardless of who performs the services, or

Expenses. (bold, underlined)

3. We agree to reimburse you for expenses as follows:

make all letter items bullets and indented

   A. Travel by Car: .40 cents per mile.
   B. Travel by Air or Train: The actual cost of the round-trip ticket.
   C. Expenses associated with photography, reproduction of documents and photography expenses, preparation of exhibits and storage of materials.
   D. Lodging: For any travel of more than 100 miles from your office, we will reimburse you for the cost of ~~room and board~~

meals and lodging

   E. Car Rental: In the event of travel beyond the local area, we will reimburse you for the cost of ~~any size~~ car rental and any associated expenses.

a mid-size

(continued)

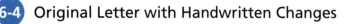

6-4   Original Letter with Handwritten Changes

We reserve the right to investigate and verify your credentials and you agree that you are qualified to perform the services outlined in this letter agreement.

You will issue us bills on a monthly basis or whatever other interval deemed appropriate by both parties. Bills will be paid upon receipt and will be deemed delinquent if not paid within 30 days of the date of issuance. Interest shall accrue on any delinquent balance at the maximum rate permitted by law. ~~not to exceed 1.5 percent per month.~~ In the event we do not pay your bill for 60 days or more from the date of issuance, you will have the unrestricted right to resign from performing additional services in this matter for the firm.

*

Your signature below represents your agreement with the terms set forth herein. Please return a signed copy of this letter to my office and we will issue a check for your engagement fee.

Sincerely,
Mary Ellen Janetti

*Add paragraph: This agreement shall be interpreted under the laws of the state of Florida. Any litigation that results under this agreement shall be resolved in the trial courts of Broward County, Florida.

I accept the terms of this agreement.

_____
Signature of Expert

_____
Date

(concluded)

Critical Thinking

When serving a defendant with suit papers, what are the advantages and disadvantages of using:

1. the county sheriff's office?

2. a private process server?

Preparation of Real Estate Documents

From Attorney Davis

We have recently opened a file for our new client, Jolinda Green. She is the daughter and personal representative of the late Melvin Green, and she will be acting in that capacity for the sale of his home to the buyer, Camilla Crabtree. I have left the New Client Information Sheet on your desk to use in preparing the documents.

She has hired us to handle the closing for the home, but we have found a minor defect in the title that needs to be cleared before proceeding with this transaction. Therefore, I have dictated an engagement letter to Ms. Green as well as the first draft of a quiet title suit for you to prepare using our standard pleading format, with the rest of the paperwork to be completed later. I also want to prepare a few of the closing documents ahead of time, so please prepare the warranty deed, bill of sale, and a no-lien affidavit using our standard forms. She left with us a copy of the legal description of the property from her father's title insurance policy, which is measured in metes and bounds. She also gave us a list of the personal property that will be conveyed to the buyer when preparing the bill of sale.

Finally, I have dictated a pre-closing checklist I would like to start using for our real estate transactions, since we will start issuing title insurance policies soon, as an added service to our clients. Thank you.

tasks

7-1 Prepare client engagement letter

7-2 Prepare Quiet Title Complaint

7-3 Prepare Warranty Deed

7-4 Prepare Bill of Sale

7-5 Prepare No-Lien Affidavit

7-6 Prepare pre-closing checklist

Prepare Client Engagement Letter

Open the **LETTERHEAD** file. Then open the dictation file **T7-1 ENGAGE-MENT LETTER**. Using the New Client Information Sheet (Figure 7-1), transcribe the document dictated by Attorney Davis. Upon completion, save the letter as **T7-1 GREEN-LETTER** and print.

Prepare Quiet Title Complaint

Refer to the Office Procedures Manual for the format, style, and other information used when preparing complaints and other pleadings for the firm. From the Transcription CD, open the dictation file **T7-2 QUIET TITLE** dictation file. Transcribe and prepare the Complaint to Quiet Title. Upon completion, save the document as **T7-2 GREEN-COMPLAINT** and print.

MACROS—Create a macro to insert the legal description repetitively in documents. Click Tools/Macro/Record New Macro.

Prepare Warranty Deed

Refer to the Office Procedures Manual to study the format, style, and other information when preparing real estate documents for the firm. Open the file **WARRDEED**, which is the blank warranty deed form used by the firm. Use the information contained in this scenario and refer to the copy of the legal description provided by Ms. Green (Figure 7-3) to prepare the warranty deed. Insert the required information into the appropriate bracketed places in the document. Upon completion, save the document as **T7-3 GREEN-WDEED** and print one copy.

7-1   New Client Information Sheet for Jolinda Green

REAL ESTATE CLIENT INFORMATION SHEET

Responsible Attorney (Initials):   **RJD**   Date: (date of this project)

Name of Client: **JOLINDA GREEN**   SSN: **555-12-1234**
Name on Deed: **JOLINDA GREEN, as personal representative of the estate
of MELVIN GREEN, deceased.**

Client's Address: **1447 Pleasantview Drive
Plantation, Florida 33321-8882**

Phone Numbers: Home: **(954) 555-0138**   Work: **(954) 555-0103**

Name of BUYER: **CAMILLA CRABTREE**   SSN: **555-77-3456**
Name on Deed: **CAMILLA CRABTREE, a single woman.**

BUYER'S Address: **550 Hancock Road
Fort Lauderdale, Florida 33316-2660**

Phone Numbers: Home: **(954) 555-0147**   Work: **(954) 555-0121**

Buyer's Attorney: **Harold J. Flynn, Esq.
876 Ocean Avenue
Miami, Florida 33131-4500**

PROPERTY INFORMATION

Legal Description: **See separate sheet furnished by client.**

Property Address: **6225 Palm Circle, Fort Lauderdale, Florida 33301-3229.**

Joint-Survivorship clause in Deed?   **No**

SELLING PRICE: $ _225,000.00_

How is it to be paid?   _Cashier's Check_   (CASH?) (CASHIER'S CHECK?)

Funds to be placed in escrow?   _Yes_   Whose? Buyer's Attorney

Last Appraisal Date: _April 1952_
Appraised Value: _$9,500.00_   **CLIENT TO BRING COPY TO ATTORNEY.**

Ernest Money Contract? _Yes_   Amount of deposit by Buyer: $ _20,000.00_

Is there to be a new survey made?   _Yes_   If so, by whom? Surveyor Chosen by Buyer

Who to pay for survey?   _Buyer_

Legal Description of Property

> ALTA OWNER'S POLICY
> CONTINUATION SHEET…
>
> LEGAL DESCRIPTION OF PROPERTY:
>
>
> BEGINNING at a corner post in the west margin of Maple Road, said post being the most southerly corner of the Melvin Green property as appears in Official Records Book 229, Page 772, in the Public Records of Broward County, Florida, and the most southeast corner of property of Mrs. Emee Lou Johnson as appears in Official Records Book 81, Page 520, of the Public Records of Broward County Florida, and continuing as follows: N 4 deg. 07 min. 08 sec., E 576.19 feet to an iron pin, the corner to Melvin Green, S 74 deg. 48 min 10 sec., E 476.47 feet to an iron pin, in the west margin of Maple Road, thence with the said margins S 31 deg. 13 min. 29 sec., W 114.97 feet to a point at the beginning of a curve to the right, thence with the said curve having a radius of 729.30 feet and a long chord of S 46 deg 33 min 37 sec., W 385.76 feet to a point in the said margin, thence S 61 deg. 53 min. 45 sec., W 183.08 feet to the point of beginning containing 3.72 acres, as per survey by Jack L. Smooth, RLS, whose address is 9500 Beachfront Avenue, Fort Lauderdale, Florida.

Prepare Bill of Sale

Open the file **BILL-OF-SALE**, which is the blank bill of sale form used by the firm. Use the information contained on this form and refer to the copy of the legal description provided by Ms. Green (Figure 7-3) and the handwritten list of personal property items to be conveyed (Figure 7-4), to prepare the bill of sale by inserting the required information into the appropriate places in the document. Upon completion, save the document as **T7-4 GREEN-BILLSALE** and print.

7-4 Handwritten List of Personal Property from Jolinda Green

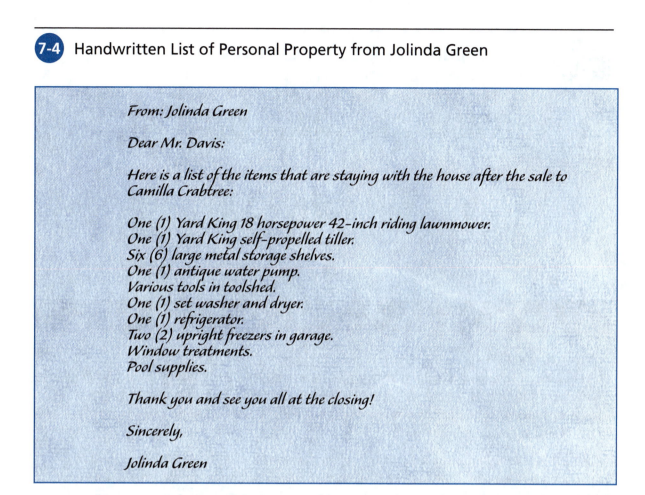

From: Jolinda Green

Dear Mr. Davis:

Here is a list of the items that are staying with the house after the sale to Camilla Crabtree:

One (1) Yard King 18 horsepower 42-inch riding lawnmower.
One (1) Yard King self-propelled tiller.
Six (6) large metal storage shelves.
One (1) antique water pump.
Various tools in toolshed.
One (1) set washer and dryer.
One (1) refrigerator.
Two (2) upright freezers in garage.
Window treatments.
Pool supplies.

Thank you and see you all at the closing!

Sincerely,

Jolinda Green

Prepare No-Lien Affidavit

7-5

Open the file **NOLIEN-AFF**, which is the no-lien affidavit form used by the firm. Use the information contained on this form and refer to the copy of the legal description provided by Ms. Green (Figure 7-3) to prepare the no-lien affidavit by inserting the required information into the appropriate places in the document. Upon completion, save the document as **T7-5 GREEN-NOLIEN** and print one copy of the affidavit.

7-6

Prepare Pre-Closing Checklist

Open the dictation file **T7-6 CHECKLIST**. Transcribe the pre-closing checklist dictated by Attorney Davis in a table format. Upon completion, save the document as **T7-6 PRECLOSING-CHECKLIST** and print.

LEGAL FOCUS

Protecting a Title

At closing, a seller warrants good title of a property to the buyer, free of liens and encumbrances. Title insurance ensures that title is indeed "good," and protects the buyer against hidden loss or damages due to a previously unknown claim of interest on the property that may come to light later.

Before issuing title insurance, a title company will conduct an ownership search of the property in question, called a "chain of title." Residential property often has a long and convoluted history of previous owners and transactions, some going back to the first issue of land by the government to early settlers. The title search uncovers any title defects such as unpaid mortgages, judgments, or any restrictions limiting the use of the land. Any issues, or "clouds" on the title, are either fixed before issuing the title policy or the coverage is specifically written to exclude those items. Standard coverage exceptions include unrecorded mechanic's liens, boundary line disputes, or claims of people living on the property not on the public record (squatters).

Some defects not revealed by a title search could include hidden hazards involving fraud, name confusion, or clerical errors in the county records that would result in a possible claim against the title for which a new owner would be responsible. In those instances, a "quiet title suit" is brought to petition the court to cancel a claim that could affect ownership of title and to declare a person's ownership in the real estate free and clear.

Critical Thinking

In the law, "attractive nuisance" is the term used to describe a potentially harmful object so inviting or interesting to a child that it would attract him or her onto one's property to investigate, leaving a homeowner liable for the child's injury or death. List some items or situations that might be considered an attractive nuisance around a typical home and the steps a homeowner could take to prevent harm to children who may be drawn to those objects.

Preparation of Discovery Documents

From Attorney Haynes

I am ready to complete some of the discovery documents in the Carmella Ruiz case. On your desk is a copy of the answer filed in this case for you to refer to for the case number and the defendant's attorney information.

First I have dictated a set of interrogatories for the defendant, as well as a request for admissions. Then my paralegal has scheduled the deposition of the plaintiff's physician, Dr. Bishop, for October 13 at 5:00 p.m., at his office located at 300 Professional Plaza, Boca Raton, Florida 33433-2200. Please prepare a notice of taking deposition and subpoena duces tecum for the doctor so he may produce our client's medical records for us at the deposition. The language in the duces tecum portion of the subpoena should request the doctor to bring the following: any and all medical records; reports; notes; X-rays; memoranda; charts; billing information; and any and all other information pertaining to the patient, Carmella Ruiz. I would like Prime Time Process Service to issue and serve the subpoena on the doctor, so please prepare a check request accordingly. I have also dictated a letter to Dr. Bishop about the deposition. Please leave the documents on my desk for my signature. Thanks.

tasks

8-1 Prepare Interrogatories

8-2 Prepare Request for Admissions

8-3 Prepare Notice of Taking Deposition

8-4 Prepare Subpoena for Deposition Duces Tecum

8-5 Prepare check request

8-6 Prepare letter to plaintiff's physician

Prepare Interrogatories

1. Open the form file **INTERROG-FORM**, which is the form for preparing interrogatories for the firm. Refer to the defendant's answer (Figure 8-1) to obtain the court heading, case number, case name, and defendant's attorney's name and address for the certificate of service at the end of the notice.

2. Open the dictation file **T8-1 INTERROGATORIES**, which is the form for preparing interrogatories for the firm. Transcribe and prepare the pleading as dictated by Attorney Haynes. Upon completion, save the document as **T8-1 RUIZ-INTERROGS** and print one copy of the interrogatories.

Prepare Request for Admissions

Open the dictation file **T8-2 ADMISSIONS** and refer to the defendant's answer (Figure 8-1) to obtain and prepare the court heading, case number, case name, and defendant's attorney's name and address for the certificate of service at the end of the notice in a blank document window. Transcribe the pleading as dictated by Attorney Haynes as a new document. Upon completion, save the document as **T8-2 RUIZ-REQFORADM** and print one copy of the request for admissions.

Prepare Notice of Taking Deposition

Open the file **NOTICE-DEP**, which is the notice of taking deposition form used by the firm. Refer to the defendant's answer (Figure 8-1) to obtain the court heading, case number, case name, and defendant's attorney's name and address for the certificate of service at the end of the notice. Use the information contained on this form to prepare the notice by inserting the required information into the appropriate places in the document. Upon completion, save the notice as **T8-3 BISHOP-NDEPO** and print.

8-1 Answer of Defendant

IN THE CIRCUIT COURT OF THE
17TH JUDICIAL CIRCUIT IN AND
FOR BROWARD COUNTY, FLORIDA

CASE NO: 2X-12345-CV

CARMELLA RUIZ,

      Plaintiff,

v.

CINDY LONG,

      Defendant.
_____/

ANSWER

      Defendant, CINDY LONG, by and through her undersigned attorney, responds to the Complaint of the Plaintiff, CARMELLA RUIZ, as follows:

      1. The Defendant is without knowledge as to the allegations of paragraph 1, and therefore, neither admits nor denies the same but demands strict proof thereof.

      2. As to this Defendant, the allegations contained in paragraph 2 are admitted.

      3. The Defendant admits the allegations in paragraph 3.

      I HEREBY CERTIFY that a true copy of the foregoing was furnished by mail this _____day of_____, 20XX, to William T. Haynes, Esq., Reginald J. Davis and Associates, Attorney for Plaintiff, 1200 N.E. First Avenue, Suite 500, Fort Lauderdale, FL 33316-1157.

_____
JOSEPH T. STERN, ESQ.
Attorney for Defendant
1200 Parkway Towers
4250 Atlantic Avenue
Pompano Beach, Florida 33064-4301
Phone: (954) 555-0167
Fax: (954) 555-0166

Prepare Subpoena for Deposition Duces Tecum

Open the file **SUBP-DT**, which is the blank subpoena duces tecum form used by the firm. Use the information contained in this scenario and refer to the defendant's answer to prepare the subpoena by inserting the required information into the appropriate places in the document. Upon completion, save the document as **T8-4 BISHOP-SUBDT** and print one copy of it.

Prepare Check Request

Open the file **CHECKREQ**. Refer to the Office Procedures Manual to locate the address of Prime Time Process Servers and the price charged by the company for service of a subpoena duces tecum. Complete the check request for the amount required. Upon completion, save the check request as **T8-5-RUIZ DEPOCHECK** and print.

Prepare Letter to Plaintiff's Physician

Open the file **LETTERHEAD**. Then open the dictation file **T8-6 BISHOP LETTER**. Transcribe the letter to the plaintiff's physician dictated by attorney Haynes. Upon completion, save the letter as **T8-6 BISHOP-LTR** and print.

L E G A L   F O C U S

Automated Docketing Systems

Law firms used to keep their calendars of important dates manually. In litigation, this was a complex process because certain key events, such as a trial date, prompted other related dates and deadlines. Using paper calendars, calculators, or counting fingers to manually count off days and mark deadlines was time consuming and subject to error, especially when dates had to be recalculated when dates for depositions, hearings, or trials changed.

To save time and alleviate potential malpractice claims because of missed dates, law firms now use automated calendaring systems. Collectively called "docket management systems," these programs differ from a typical electronic calendar, which is simply a digitized version of a paper calendar and still requires manual entries. A docket management program automatically schedules all relevant dates in a case. For example, a trial date can be entered and the program will schedule all the other important related deadlines that go with it, even calculating due dates around local holiday lists. The program provides automatic reminders, and even recalculates an entire set of due dates when one date changes, on all calendars for everyone in the firm. The program can also automatically verify names of clients to ensure that scheduling changes are applied to the right case, preventing users from making errors by misidentifying clients with similar names. Inasmuch as missed deadlines and dates account for more than 40 percent of all legal malpractice claims, most insurance carriers now give premium discounts to firms that use an automated docket calendaring program.

The use of sophisticated docketing programs will become even more commonplace as law firms strive to save time and money, to reduce the risk of malpractice claims due to missed deadlines by automating one of the most important tasks performed in the office.

Critical Thinking

Depositions and interrogatories are two of the most frequently used methods of obtaining discovery in a litigation matter. Discuss the differences between these two discovery methods and in which situations one method would be more beneficial than the other.

Preparation of Criminal Defense Documents

From Attorney Lee

We have been asked to represent Joseph Myers in his arrest on drug possession charges. Please create the New Client Information Sheet and the conflict of interest paperwork for the staff using my handwritten notes. Then prepare our standard notice of appearance, written plea of not guilty, and demand for discovery in the case using the forms on our computer. I have also dictated a motion to suppress evidence for the client. Finally, I have written down some ideas for a trifold informational brochure to give to our new clients in a criminal matter. Please prepare a rough draft of this brochure for my review.

PHOTO: © Jack Star/PhotoLink/Getty Images

tasks

9-1 Prepare New Client Information Sheet

9-2 Prepare conflict of interest paperwork

9-3 Prepare Notice of Appearance

9-4 Prepare Written Plea of Not Guilty

9-5 Prepare Demand for Discovery

9-6 Prepare Motion to Suppress

9-7 Prepare client brochure

Prepare New Client Information Sheet

Open the **CLIENT-INFO-CRIM** form. Use the information contained in Attorney Lee's handwritten notes in Figure 9-1 and insert the required information into the form. Upon completion, save the document as **T9-1 MYERS-INFO** and print.

9-1 Handwritten New Client Note

Client: Joey Myers (age 53) Nicknames: "Huggy" Myers, Joseph Myers, J.J. Daddy.
Wife's name: Tina Marie Myers (maiden name Nicholson)
1159 Hickory Trace Drive
Plantation, Florida 33320-9900
Home phone: (954) 555-0104   Work: (954) 555-0137   Cell phone: (954) 555-0144
DOB: 1/4/52 (a 25-year Army veteran)
Date of Arrest: July 3, 20XX

Drug charge—client was arrested last Saturday night on Oak Hill Blvd. after selling 1 ounce of cocaine to undercover cop for Fort Lauderdale Police Dept. Client arrested and charged with possession and intent to sell. Has not bonded out at this time. Client's auto seized and impounded. Arraignment tomorrow morning.

Location of incident: 549 Oak Hill Blvd., Ft. Laud., at 11:30 p.m. (in front of Foodway Market)

Client's employer: OHarry's Appliance Center, as a salesman.

Fee – hourly plus $5,000 retainer

Need to Do:

* Open new file – retainer letter.
* Get police report – Ft. Lauderdale P.D. and arrest record.
* Prepare initial pleadings. State Attorney: Daniel Murowski, Esq.

Prepare Conflict of Interest Paperwork

1. Open the file **COI-FORM**. Use the information contained in Attorney Lee's handwritten notes and insert the required information at the top and in the Criminal section of the form. Upon completion, save the document as **T9-2 MYERS-COIFORM** and print.
2. Open the **COI-MEMO** form. Insert the required information regarding the new client. Upon completion, save the memo as **T9-2 MYERS-COIMEMO** and print.

Prepare Notice of Appearance

Open the **NOTICE-APPEARANCE** file. Use the information contained in Attorney Lee's handwritten notes and the state's Information document in Figure 9-3 to insert the appropriate court heading and names of parties. Insert the required information in the body of the pleading and in the certificate of service. Add a firm signature line for Attorney Lee's signature. Upon completion, save the notice as **T9-3 MYERS-NOAP** and print.

Prepare Written Plea of Not Guilty

Open the **NOT-GUILTY-PLEA** form. Use the information contained in Attorney Lee's handwritten notes and the Information document to insert the required information into the pleading and certificate of service. Add a firm signature line for Attorney Lee's signature. Upon completion, save the document as **T9-4 MYERS-NOTGUILTY** and print.

L E G A L   F O C U S

Victim Compensation

In some instances, convicted defendants are forced to pay restitution to the victim of a crime. The purpose of restitution is to compensate the victim for losses that he or she suffered as a result of the crime or to rehabilitate the defendant, for example, if probation is conditioned on payment of restitution to the victim. Restitution covers only out-of-pocket expenses incurred by a victim as a result of the crime, and some jurisdictions limit the amount of restitution a victim may recover from a criminal proceeding. Restitution also does not compensate a victim for physical pain or emotional trauma. For these types of claims, a victim must seek remedy in a civil action against the defendant.

Information

IN THE CIRCUIT COURT OF THE
17TH JUDICIAL CIRCUIT IN AND
FOR BROWARD COUNTY, FLORIDA

CASE NO.: 2X-9400 DIVISION "J"

STATE OF FLORIDA,

INFORMATION FOR:

    Plaintiff,

vs.

VIOLATION OF FLORIDA COMPREHENSIVE
DRUG ABUSE PREVENTION AND CONTROL
JOSEPH A. MYERS,

ACT (Sale of Counterfeit Drug) 30

    Defendant.
_____/

IN THE NAME AND BY THE AUTHORITY OF THE STATE OF FLORIDA:

DANIEL MUROWSKI, ESQ., state attorney for the above-captioned Court, prosecuting for the State of Florida, in the said County, under oath, states that:

JOSEPH A. MYERS

of the county of Broward and state of Florida, on the 25th day of June, in the year of our Lord, two thousand_____(20XX), in the county and state aforesaid,

        did agree, consent, or offer to sell to another person, an
        undercover police officer, a certain controlled substance, to wit:
        Cocaine, and did thereafter sell to said person said controlled
        substance....

contrary to Chapter 817.563(1) , Florida Statutes, and against the peace and dignity of the state of Florida.

STATE OF FLORIDA
                  SS:
COUNTY OF BROWARD

Before me personally appeared DANIEL MUROWSKI, the undersigned state attorney for the above-captioned Court, or his duly designated assistant state attorney, who being first duly sworn, says that the allegations set forth in the foregoing Information are based upon facts that have been sworn to as true, and which if true, would constitute the offense therein charged; hence this Information document is filed in good faith in instituting this prosecution, and that testimony was received under oath from a material witness or witnesses.

                        _____
                        Assistant State Attorney for the
                        above-captioned Court, prosecuting
                        for said State

      Sworn to and subscribed before me this_____ day of _____, 20XX.

                        _____
                        Notary Public

My Commission Expires:

Prepare Demand for Discovery

Open the **DEMAND-FOR-DISCOVERY** form. Use the information contained in Attorney Lee's handwritten notes and the Information document to insert the required information into the body of the pleading and certificate of service. Add a firm signature line for Attorney Lee's signature. Upon completion, save the document as **T9-5 MYERS-DISCOVERY** and print.

Prepare Motion to Suppress

1. Open the dictation file **T9-6 SUPPRESS**. Refer to the state's Information document to key the court heading.
2. Listen to the Transcription CD and transcribe the motion dictated by Attorney Lee as a new document. Upon completion, save the motion as **T9-6 MYERS-MSUPPRESS** and print.

Prepare Client Brochure

1. Refer to Attorney Lee's drawing in Figure 9-7 to study his ideas for a new client brochure.
2. Open the **C-BROCHURE** file, which is a basic trifold form for a three-panel brochure with markers indicating the top of each panel and type of information to be inserted.
3. Delete the marker text and insert the required text into the respective panels of the brochure. Use creative features such as different font styles, sizes, and colors to format the text. Add appropriate clip art images where indicated. Use Wingdings font, shading, and/or borders to create a professional brochure. Use color and texture from the Drawing toolbar to place a rectangle around the data entry area and apply a texture to parts of the brochure. Upon completion, save the brochure as **T9-7 CLIENT-BROCHURE** and print one copy.

DRAWING TOOLBAR—To view the Drawing toolbar, click View, Toolbars, Drawing.

9-7 Handwritten Drawing of Criminal Law Brochure

Back panel of brochure

DO YOU NEED AN ATTORNEY?

As your attorneys, we will offer you exceptional legal presentation for your criminal defense at a cost you can afford.

Back of brochure...

THE FOCUS IS ON YOU!

CALL US FOR A FREE CONSULTATION
Appointments at your convenience, days or evenings.

IF YOU ARE ARRESTED, CALL US IMMEDIATELY!

24-HOUR EMERGENCY HOTLINE:
1-800-555-0101

Nice little clip art here....

Put our firm name, address telephone, and fax here

Outside cover here...

REGINALD J. DAVIS & ASSOCIATES
ATTORNEYS AND COUNSELORS AT LAW......

Put nice legal type clip art here.

Inside panel #1:

OUTSTANDING EXPERIENCE

Our attorneys are law specialists serving our clients for over 25 years. We collectively have over 200 years of criminal trial court experience. Our firm is well versed in the rules of criminal procedure and highly regarded in the legal community. We are here to advise, comfort, challenge, and protect.

OUR STAFF:

List the names of our attorneys here.

Inside panel #2

AREAS OF CRIMINAL PRACTICE

We defend the rights of clients charged with a variety of offenses, handling issues involving:

*Misdemeanors and felonies
* DUI
*Domestic violence
*Drug charges
*Traffic violations
*Probation violations
*Federal offenses
*Theft and burglary
*Expungement
*Criminal appeals and writs
*Assault and battery
*White-collar crimes

Inside panel #3:

IF YOU ARE ARRESTED:

1. Keep silent. Do not talk to anyone about the alleged crime until you speak to an attorney. More people talk their way into jail than out of jail.

2. Get an attorney. You have the right to an attorney. If you cannot afford one, the court will appoint a public defender for you.

3. Do not post a high bail. It may be possible to reduce your bail or have you released without paying bail early in the proceedings.

4. Do not disappear. Make sure you know when your court dates are and that you don't miss court appearances. If you miss an appearance, your bail is recalled and you may have to spend more time in jail.

Critical Thinking

Call or visit your local courthouse to find out the current rules in effect regarding the filing of pleadings electronically. Discuss your findings as well as the effect of e-filing on client confidentiality and timeliness of filing, and the advantages or disadvantages of using an e-filing system to file pleadings and other documents with the court.

Preparation of Trial Documents

From Attorney Haynes

The court has noticed the Ruiz case for the two-week trial docket commencing November 1, 20XX before Judge Matthew Drake. Please prepare the joint pretrial stipulation and exhibit list I have dictated. I have also dictated jury instructions and a verdict form. In addition, Dana Priest has left a memo on your desk containing the information you will need to prepare the trial subpoenas to be issued. Finally, please prepare a letter to the witnesses with instructions about the trial, which I have dictated.

tasks

10-1 Prepare Joint Pretrial Stipulation

10-2 Prepare Pretrial Exhibit List

10-3 Prepare Jury Instructions

10-4 Prepare Verdict Form

10-5 Prepare trial subpoenas

10-6 Prepare merge letter to witnesses

Prepare Joint Pretrial Stipulation

Open the **JOINT-STIP** form. Then open the dictation file **T10-1 STIPULA-TION**. Listen to the dictation and prepare the pleading dictated by Attorney Haynes. Upon completion, save the document as **T10-1 RUIZ-STIP** and print.

Prepare Pretrial Exhibit List

Open the dictation file **T10-2 EXHIBITS**. Listen to the dictation and transcribe the pleading as dictated by Attorney Haynes as a new document. Upon completion, save the exhibit list as **T10-2 RUIZ-EXHLIST** and print.

Prepare Jury Instructions

Open the dictation file **T10-3 JURY**. Listen and transcribe the jury instructions as dictated by Attorney Haynes as a new document. Upon completion, save the document as **T10-3 RUIZ-JURYINST** and print.

Prepare Verdict Form

Open the dictation file **T10-4 VERDICT FORM**. Listen and transcribe the verdict form dictated by Attorney Haynes as a new document. Upon completion, save the form as **T10-4 RUIZ-VERDICT** and print.

Prepare Trial Subpoenas

Open the **TRIAL-SUBP** form. Use the information contained in Dana Priest's witness list memo in Figure 10-5 to prepare the trial subpoenas for the witnesses in the case, inserting the required information in the form for each trial subpoena. Upon completion, save each document as follows and print one copy of each subpoena.

Dr. Samuel Bishop: **T10-5 RUIZ-BISHOP-SUBPDT**

Gerald Simms, PT: **T10-5 RUIZ-SIMMS-SUBPDT**

Officer Mario Marcone,
  Fort Lauderdale Police Dept.: **T10-5 RUIZ-MARCONE-SUBDT**

Records Custodian,
  County Ambulance Service: **T10-5 RUIZ-COUNTY-SUBDT**

Records Custodian,
  Doctor's Medical Center: **T10-5 RUIZ-DOCTORS-SUBDT**

Records Custodian,
  Bud's Pink Flamingo Factory: **T10-5 RUIZ-BUDS-SUBDT**

LEGAL FOCUS

LOA's role in pretrial preparation

The final days of trial preparation can be stressful for both attorney and staff. Before trial, a legal office assistant helps to organize and maintain important files and exhibits so that they are readily accessible in the courtroom. During a trial, a legal office assistant coordinates schedules and appearances of witnesses and serves as a central contact person at the office for the attorney. He or she can also monitor deadlines, hand-deliver supplies and other items to the courthouse for use by the attorney, prepare documents needed immediately, and assist all the other members of the legal team involved in the trial. The legal office assistant plays a vital role in the trial preparation process, assists the attorney in maintaining focus and perspective, and helps eliminate the need for frantic last-minute pretrial preparation.

Reginald J. Davis and Associates

MEMORANDUM

TO: (Student's Name)

FROM: Dana Priest

DATE: (Current Date)

SUBJECT: Ruiz v. Long
Trial Subpoena Information

Here is the list I have so far of witnesses we will call at trial, for you to use in preparing the pretrial pleadings and trial subpoenas. For the trial subpoenas, I have written down what each party is to bring to the trial, where required. Let me know if you need anything else. Thanks.

Dr. Samuel Bishop
300 Professional Plaza
Boca Raton, FL 33433-2200
Any and all medical records, reports, notes, X-rays, memoranda, charts, billing information, and any and all other information pertaining to the patient, Carmella Ruiz.

Gerald Simms, PT
ABC Physical Therapy
9130 Medical Centre Drive
Suite 2200
For Simms subpoena:
Any and all medical records, reports, notes, X-rays, memoranda, charts, billing information, and any and all other information pertaining to the patient, Carmella Ruiz.

Officer Mario Marcone
Fort Lauderdale Police Department
1300 West Broward Blvd.
Fort Lauderdale, FL 33312-1311
Any and all records or reports concerning that certain traffic accident involving (names of parties) which occurred on (date), more particularly described as Accident Report No. 2X-12345.

Records Custodian
County Ambulance Service
1620 North Andrews Avenue
Fort Lauderdale, Florida 33130-3855
Any and all transportation records concerning that certain traffic accident involving (names of parties) which occurred on (date).

Records Custodian
Doctor's Medical Center
5600 Independence Way
Fort Lauderdale, FL 33322-4955
Any and all medical records, reports, notes, X-rays, memoranda, charts, billing information, and any and all other information pertaining to the patient, Carmella Ruiz.

Records Custodian
Bud's Pink Flamingo Factory
450 Davie Road
Davie, Florida 33312-3822
Fort Lauderdale, Florida 33316-8220
Any and all records that comprise your entire employment/personnel file regarding CINDY LONG, including but not limited to employment application, physical exam reports, payroll and attendance reports, and any and all records concerning job performance.

Prepare Merge Letter to Witnesses

1. Open the dictation file **T10-6 MERGE LETTER**. Transcribe the form letter dictated by Attorney Haynes. Upon completion, save the letter as **T10-6 RUIZ-MERGELETTER** and print.

2. Use the information contained in Dana Priest's witness memo (Figure 10-5) to prepare the data file of names and addresses to be used for the merge letter.
3. Merge the data file with the form letter. Upon completion, save the entire merged letter document as **T10-6 RUIZ-TRIAL LETTERS** and print one copy of each letter.

MAIL MERGE—Use Mail Merge to create form letters. Click Tools, Letters and Mailings, Mail Merge.

Critical Thinking

When preparing for trial, many attorneys like to have materials and important information they will need while in court organized into a large black binder called a "trial notebook." Discuss what items you would place in such a book and how you would organize that information so that the attorney or paralegal can easily retrieve it as necessary during the course of the trial.

Preparation of Corporate Documents

From Attorney Janetti

Our landscaper, Jimmy Holmes, and his two friends, Wendell Snow and Joe Butler, want to form a new corporation called Three Guys Landscaping, Inc. Prepare the articles of incorporation for the new business, as well as the other documents needed to start the corporation, using the information contained in my notes and the forms on our computer. I have also dictated the letter to the secretary of state to file the articles of incorporation. Then prepare a bill for the $750 flat fee for our legal services, plus the cost for the filing fee, with a cover letter to the client, which I have dictated.

tasks

11-1   Prepare Articles of Incorporation

11-2   Prepare letter to secretary of state

11-3   Prepare organizational meeting minutes

11-4   Prepare corporation bylaws

11-5   Prepare stock certificates

11-6   Prepare billing invoice

11-7   Prepare letter to client

Prepare Articles of Incorporation

Open the **ART-OF-INC** form. Use the information contained in Attorney Janetti's instructions, as well as her notes in Figure 11-1, to prepare the articles of incorporation. Insert the required information into the appropriate places in the document. Upon completion, save the document as **T11-1 HOLMES-ARTOFINC** and print.

Prepare Letter to Secretary of State

Open the **LETTERHEAD** form. Then open the dictation file **T11-2 SEC-STATE LETTER**. Transcribe the letter dictated by Attorney Janetti to the secretary of state and key an envelope. Upon completion, save the document as **T11-2 HOLMES-SECSTATE-LTR** and print one copy of the letter and envelope.

L E G A L   F O C U S

Piercing the Corporate Veil

A corporation is said to be like a "veil" that shields its shareholders from being personally responsible for corporate debts and other liabilities, such as a lawsuit. This benefit is only available, however, if the integrity of the corporation as a separate entity is respected by a court. In certain circumstances, courts may look through the corporation, called "piercing the corporate veil," and hold the shareholders personally liable for obligations of the corporation. The issue of whether the corporate veil can be pierced in terms of liability is usually determined by whether the corporation looks and acts like a corporation should. If the shareholders treat the corporation and conduct its business as a separate and legal entity, then the court will usually uphold the status of a corporation and will not find personal liability. However, if corporate formalities and document preparation and maintenance are not consistently observed, the corporation will be disregarded and the individuals may be held personally liable. Therefore, a corporation must be formed and maintained according to the letter of the law to shield its shareholders from personal liability for its debts.

11-1   Corporation Information Sheet

NEW CLIENT INFORMATION SHEET

Name of corporation: _____ *Three Guys Landscaping, Inc.* _____
Name of incorporator: _____ *James A. Holmes* _____
Date of incorporation: _____ *(Date of this project)* _____

Directors:

James A. Holmes   *248 Hidden Lake Road*
                                             Fort Lauderdale, Florida 33319-9068

Wendell Snow   *625 East Spruce Street*
                                             Plantation, Florida 33325-1139

Joseph G. Butle   *11289 Harbor Avenue*
                                             Fort Lauderdale, Florida 33330-4275

Maximum number of directors: _____ *3* _____
Authorized shares of common stock: _____ *3,000* _____   Par value: _____ *$1* _____

Shares to be issued:

James A. Holmes – 500 shares
Wendell Snow – 500 shares
Joseph G. Butler – 500 shares

Principal place of business: _____ *Jim's address* _____
Registered agent: _____ *Jim, at his address* _____
Annual meeting date and location: _____ *November 1 of each year, at Jim's address* _____
Fiscal year: _____ *Jan. – Dec.* _____

First meeting:

Date: _____ *November 1, 20XX, at 2 p.m.* _____
Place: _____ *Jim's address* _____
Temporary and permanent chairman/president: _____ *Jim* _____
Temporary and permanent vice president: _____ *Wendell* _____
Temporary and permanent secretary/treasurer: _____ *Joe* _____

Prepare Organizational Meeting Minutes

Open the **ORG-MINUTES** form. Use the information contained in Attorney Janetti's notes to prepare the minutes. Insert the required information into the appropriate places in the document. Upon completion, save the file as **T11-3 HOLMES-MINUTES** and print.

Prepare Corporation Bylaws

Open the **BYLAWS** form. Use the information contained in Attorney Janetti's notes to prepare the bylaws. Insert the required information into the appropriate places in the document. Upon completion, save the document as **T11-4 HOLMES-BYLAWS** and print.

Prepare Stock Certificates

Open the **STOCK-CERT** file, which is a stock certificate form used by the firm. Use the information contained in Attorney Janetti's notes to prepare a stock certificate for each stockholder of the corporation. Insert the required information into the appropriate places in the document. Upon completion, save each document as follows and print one copy of each stock certificate.

James A. Holmes:	**T11-5 HOLMES-STOCK**
Wendell Snow:	**T11-5 SNOW-STOCK**
Joseph G. Butler:	**T11-5 BUTLER-STOCK**

Prepare Billing Invoice

Open the file **BILL-FORM**. Complete the billing invoice for the client, and indicate the flat fee of $750 for the preparation of the corporation documents, and the filing fee of $250. Calculate the total amount due. Upon completion, save the invoice as **T11-6 HOLMES-BILL** and print.

Prepare Letter to Client

Open the **LETTERHEAD** form. Then open the dictation file **T11-7 CLIENT-LTR**. Transcribe the letter dictated by Attorney Janetti to the client and key an envelope. Upon completion, save the document as **T11-7 HOLMES-LTR** and print one copy of the letter and envelope.

Internet Activity

Using the Internet, locate one or more web sites that provide information about incorporating a business in your state. Review the list of sites and links for the information you are seeking and research those sites accordingly. List your results below, including the Internet sites from which you obtained your information.

Critical Thinking

Discuss the definition and the purpose of bylaws and some reasons why a corporation would be required to maintain an accurate set of bylaws.

Appellate Procedures

From Attorney Davis

We represent our client, Jeffrey Swain, in the appeal of a matter involving his prior DUI case. Please prepare the initial pleadings to start the appeals process. Then complete the appellate brief that I had dictated but was not completed by my legal office assistant. Finally, prepare a table of contents and table of authorities for the brief.

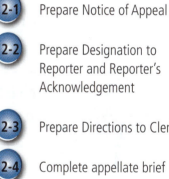

tasks

Prepare Notice of Appeal

The client, Jeffrey Swain, is appealing his DUI conviction from five years ago, in which he entered a plea of guilty on the assumption he would get his license back five years after the order was entered. It is now five years later and he recently learned that his license is revoked for life. Therefore, an appeal is being filed to vacate the original order, as Mr. Swain feels he was not fully informed of the ramifications of his plea at the time it was taken by the court. The assistant state attorney in the case at the time was Mark Malone, Esq., located at the State Attorney's Office at the Broward County Courthouse. You will prepare the notice of appeal, putting the state on notice that an appeal is being undertaken. A copy of the document will be furnished to the assistant state attorney who originally worked on the case.

Open the **NOTICE-OF-APPEAL** form. Use the information contained in the court's order in Figure 12-1 and Attorney Davis's instructions to obtain the court heading and other information you need. Prepare the notice of appeal by inserting the required information into the appropriate places in the document. Upon completion, save the form as **T12-1 SWAIN-NOTAPPEAL** and print.

Prepare Designation to Reporter and Reporter's Acknowledgement

The Designation to Reporter form is used to obtain the official court reporter's transcript of the previous proceedings. The document is prepared and, as above, a copy is sent to the assistant state attorney who originally worked on the case.

Open the **REPORTER-DESIG** form. Use the information contained in the court's order to prepare the request. Insert the required information into the appropriate places in the document. Upon completion, save the file as **T12-2 SWAIN-TRANSCRIPT** and print.

Prepare Directions to Clerk

The Directions to Clerk form outlines in detail which portions of the court file the clerk of the lower court must provide to the appellate court for review. As before, a copy is sent to the opposing counsel who originally worked on the case.

Open the **DIRECTIONS-CLERK** form. Prepare the request by inserting the required information into the appropriate places in this document. Upon completion, save the document as **T12-3 SWAIN-DIRECTIONS** and print.

12-1 Court Order

IN THE CIRCUIT COURT OF THE
17TH JUDICIAL CIRCUIT IN AND
FOR BROWARD COUNTY, FLORIDA

CASE NO.: 2X-52433 LD

STATE OF FLORIDA,

    Plaintiff,

vs.

JEFFREY SWAIN,

    Defendant.
_____/

> Clerk of the Court
> Broward County, Florida
>
> **A TRUE COPY**

ORDER ON EVIDENTIARY MOTION TO SET ASIDE JUDGMENT AND SENTENCE UNDER THE FLORIDA RULES OF CRIMINAL PROCEDURE

THIS CAUSE having come on for hearing before me upon Defendant's

Evidentiary Motion to Set Aside Judgment and Sentence Under the Florida Rules of

Criminal Procedure from a proceeding which occurred on March 29, 20XX before the

Honorable Dorothy Blackman, and the Court having considered the same and being

otherwise fully advised in the premises, it is

    ORDERED AND ADJUDGED that the said motion is hereby DENIED.

    DONE AND ORDERED in Chambers at Fort Lauderdale, Broward County,

Florida, this____15th____day of____August____, 20XX.

           _____Matthew Cannon_____
           HON. MATTHEW CANNON
           CIRCUIT COURT JUDGE

Complete Appellate Brief

Attorney Davis has dictated part of the appellate brief regarding Jeffrey Swain. You will open the partially completed brief and then complete it by transcribing the dictation in this task.

1. Refer to the Office Procedures Manual to review the format, style, and other information used when preparing appellate briefs.
2. Open the **PARTIAL-BRIEF** form. Read the brief to become familiar with the facts of the case, document formatting, and case citation style.
3. Open the dictation file **T12-4 BRIEF**. Transcribe the completion of the appellate brief dictated by Attorney Davis, following the format and style of the text and authorities that were keyed in the partial brief. Upon completion, save the brief as **T12-4 SWAIN-BRIEF** and print.

Prepare Table of Contents

1. Open the file **T12-4 SWAIN-BRIEF** created in Task 12-4. Insert a new blank page after the title page of the document. Center the title, **TABLE OF CONTENTS,** bold and underlined, at the top of the page. Double-space and key the word **PAGE** at the right margin.
2. Use the Index and Tables feature of *MS Word* to mark the items in the text of the brief that will be used in the table of contents. Locate each heading and subheading in the brief and mark it according to appropriate heading level.
3. Go back to the blank table of contents page. Click the left margin two lines beneath *PAGE* and generate the table of contents. Make style and editing changes to the heading level styles as appropriate. Upon completion, print only the table of contents page and resave the brief using the same filename.

MODIFY TOC HEADING STYLES—To edit heading styles for a table of contents, click Insert, Reference, Index and Tables. Click the Table of Contents tab, Modify, and Modify again.

Prepare Table of Authorities

1. Open the file **T12-4 SWAIN-BRIEF** that was created in Task 12-4. Create a new blank page after the table of contents page of the document. Center the title, **TABLE OF AUTHORITIES**, bold and underlined at the top of the page. Double-space and key the word **PAGE** at the right margin.

2. Use the Index and Tables feature of *MS Word* to mark the items in the text of the brief that will be used in the table of contents. Be sure to indicate the appropriate category that applies to each citation. When all the cases, statutes, rules, and other authorities have been marked and categorized, go back to the blank table of authorities' page. Click the left margin two lines beneath *PAGE* and generate the table of authorities of the brief. Make style and editing changes to the heading level styles as appropriate. Upon completion, print only the table of authorities page and resave the brief using the same filename.

SOFTWARE tip

MODIFY TABLE OF AUTHORITIES HEADING STYLES—To edit heading styles for a table of authorities, click Insert, Reference, Index and Tables. Click the Table of Authorities tab, Modify and Modify again.

Internet Activity

Use the Internet to locate one or more web sites that provide information about the U.S. District Court that serves your jurisdiction. Review the procedures, fees, and formatting particulars for the filing of appellate briefs in your state. Conduct a search for both official district court web sites for your jurisdiction or private (law firm or educational) web sites. Discuss your findings, including the Internet sites from which you obtained your information.

L E G A L   F O C U S

Avoiding Appellate Pitfalls
For many attorneys who do not normally practice in the district courts, the appellate process is a daunting journey. Failure to abide by the specific and technical requirements of the court could result in the permanent dismissal of the appeal. For example, the failure to file a *timely* notice of appeal precludes appellate review of a matter at the outset. Additionally, the failure to file a brief following all of a district's requirements, including formatting style, required sections, record excerpts, and appropriate copies, may result in automatic dismissal of the appeal. A legal office assistant, who is familiar with the rules of filing an appeal in the district court system, as well as the proper formatting requirements and mechanics of an appellate brief, will greatly aid the attorney in presenting timely, persuasive documents to the appellate court.

Critical Thinking

Can both parties in a lower court's order file an appeal of the decision at the same time? If not, why not? If so, what would the appeal by the opposing party be called?

Commencement of the Action

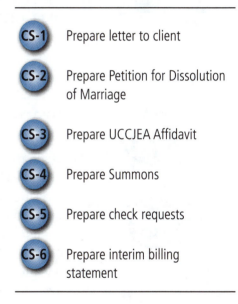

From Attorney Janetti

Please prepare some initial documents for our client, Karen Bell, in the divorce matter of Karen Bell vs. Dr. Troy Bell. First, prepare the letter of representation to the client as well as the petition for dissolution of marriage that I have dictated. Then prepare the UCCJEA affidavit and Summons for Dr. Bell, the forms of which are on our computer. Obtain the checks for the clerk's filing fee and for Justice Delivered to serve the Summons. Finally, prepare an interim bill to Karen for work done on the case to date that I have dictated.

tasks

CS-1 Prepare letter to client

CS-2 Prepare Petition for Dissolution of Marriage

CS-3 Prepare UCCJEA Affidavit

CS-4 Prepare Summons

CS-5 Prepare check requests

CS-6 Prepare interim billing statement

Prepare Letter to Client

Open the **LETTERHEAD** file. Then open the dictation file **CS1 CLIENT LETTER**. Transcribe the letter and prepare an envelope to the client dictated by Attorney Janetti. Upon completion, save as **CS1 BELL-LTR1** and print one copy of the letter and envelope.

Prepare Petition for Dissolution of Marriage

Refer to the Office Procedures Manual for the format, style, and other information used when preparing a divorce petition. Open the dictation file **CS2 DOM PETITION**. Listen and transcribe the dissolution petition dictated by Attorney Janetti. Upon completion, save the document as **CS2 BELL-DOM-PETITION** and print one copy of it.

Prepare UCCJEA Affidavit

Open the **UCCJEA-AFF** file. Using the information contained in Attorney Janetti's dictation and her notes in Figure CS-3, prepare the affidavit by inserting the required information into the appropriate places in the document. When adding information about a child into the table in this document, make sure rows do not break across pages, and create a header row if the table continues to the next page. Add rows as necessary or eliminate unused rows. Upon completion, print one copy of the UCCJEA Affidavit and save the document as **CS3 BELL-UCCJEA**.

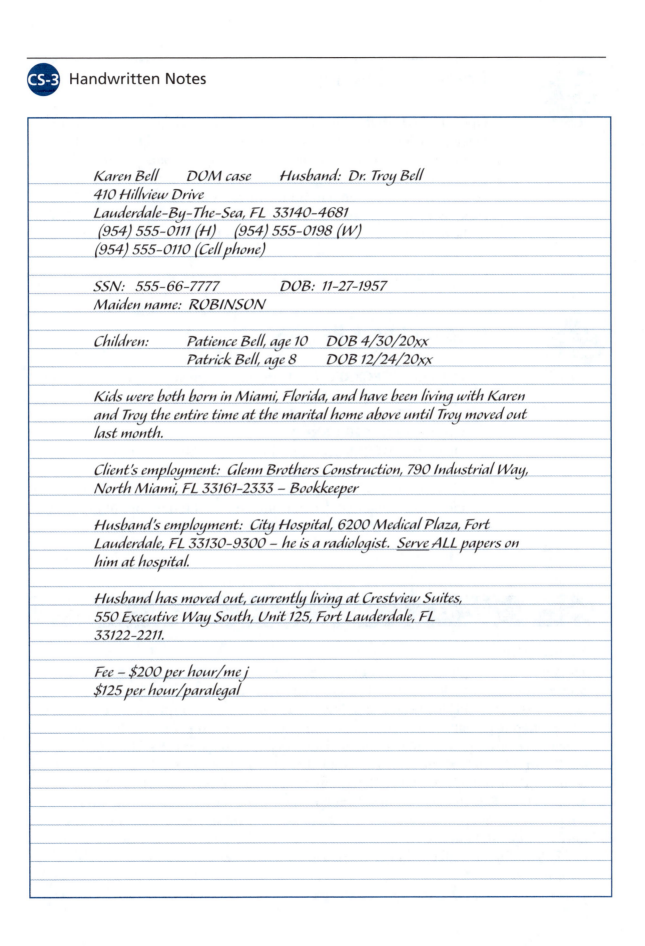

CS-3 Handwritten Notes

Karen Bell   DOM case   Husband: Dr. Troy Bell
410 Hillview Drive
Lauderdale-By-The-Sea, FL 33140-4681
 (954) 555-0111 (H)   (954) 555-0198 (W)
(954) 555-0110 (Cell phone)

SSN: 555-66-7777   DOB: 11-27-1957
Maiden name: ROBINSON

Children: Patience Bell, age 10   DOB 4/30/20xx
               Patrick Bell, age 8   DOB 12/24/20xx

Kids were both born in Miami, Florida, and have been living with Karen
and Troy the entire time at the marital home above until Troy moved out
last month.

Client's employment: Glenn Brothers Construction, 790 Industrial Way,
North Miami, FL 33161-2333 – Bookkeeper

Husband's employment: City Hospital, 6200 Medical Plaza, Fort
Lauderdale, FL 33130-9300 – he is a radiologist. Serve ALL papers on
him at hospital.

Husband has moved out, currently living at Crestview Suites,
550 Executive Way South, Unit 125, Fort Lauderdale, FL
33122-2211.

Fee – $200 per hour/me j
$125 per hour/paralegal

Prepare Summons

Open the **SUMMONS** file. Using the information contained in Attorney Janetti's dictation and her notes, prepare the Summons for Dr. Bell by inserting the required information into the appropriate places in the document. Be sure to change the words "Plaintiff" to "Petitioner" and "Defendant" to "Respondent" in the form, as this is a dissolution of marriage action as opposed to a civil action. Upon completion, print one copy of the Summons and save the document as **CS4 BELL-SUMMONS**.

Prepare Check Requests

1. Open the **CHECKREQ** file. Using the information provided by Attorney Janetti, complete the check request for the Clerk of the Court's filing fee of $350. Upon completion, print one copy of the request and save it as **BELL-CHECKREQ1**.
2. Open the **CHECKREQ** file again. Refer to the Office Procedures Manual to find the fee charged by Justice Delivered, Inc. to serve the Summons on Dr. Bell. Complete the check request for Justice Delivered for the amount required. Upon completion, print one copy of the request and save it as **CS5 BELL-CHECKREQ2**.

L E G A L   F O C U S

The UCCJEA
The Child Custody Jurisdiction and Enforcement Act (UCCJEA) governs the rules and procedures regarding determination of child custody both before and after a divorce action in order to avoid jurisdiction competition with other states. For instance, if a child is living with one parent in California and then relocates with that parent to Maine, the issue for a court is to determine whether it still has jurisdiction over that child, i.e., whether it still can hear the case. The idea behind the UCCJEA is simply that if there is a home state, then that state should determine the custody of the child. The UCCJEA prioritizes which state should have jurisdiction to resolve the dispute. It also simplifies enforcement of child custody orders when two states are involved, in an effort to speed up the execution of those types of orders. Because of this law, a UCCJEA affidavit is required to be filed with the initial petition in every case where minor children of the parties are involved.

Prepare Interim Billing Statement

1. Open the **BILL-FORM** file. Key the client's name and address and current date in the appropriate places on the document.
2. Open the dictation file **CS6 INTERIM BILL**. Listen and key the interim billing statement as dictated by Attorney Janetti. Credit the client for the funds advanced dictated by Attorney Janetti, and then calculate the final amount due from the client. Upon completion, print one copy of the document and save it as **CS6 BELL-BILL1**.

Internet Activity

Using the Internet, locate one or more web sites that provide information about the concept of no-fault divorce, the purpose of this type of divorce, the terminology used, and the states that permit no-fault divorce proceedings. Review the list of sites and links for the information you are seeking and research those sites accordingly. Discuss your findings, including the Internet sites from which you obtained your information.

Critical Thinking

When would it be prudent, or even feasible, for a couple to obtain a divorce without representation by an attorney? Why or why not?

Discovery Procedures

From Attorney Janetti

To initiate discovery in this case, please prepare our standard dissolution of marriage interrogatories and request for production to the respondent. Then prepare a motion to terminate the temporary custody agreement of the parties that I have dictated, along with a notice of hearing for two weeks from today on Judge George Nixon's 8:30 a.m. motion calendar. Finally, I have dictated an interim bill for the client. There are still some retainer funds available from the first billing, so please start with that and come up with a balance due.

tasks

CS-7 Prepare Interrogatories

CS-8 Prepare Request for Production

CS-9 Prepare Motion to Terminate Temporary Custody Agreement

CS-10 Prepare Notice of Hearing

CS-11 Prepare interim billing statement

Prepare Interrogatories

Open the file **DOM-INTERROGS**. Using the information contained in this document and the respondent's answer in Figure CS-7, prepare the pleading by inserting the required information into the appropriate places in the document. Upon completion, save as **CS7BELL-INTERROGS** and print one copy of the interrogatories.

Prepare Request for Production

Open the **DOM-REQ-PROD** file. Using the information contained in the document and the respondent's answer, prepare the pleading by inserting the required information into the appropriate places in the document. Upon completion, save as **CS8 BELL-REQ-PROD** and print one copy of it.

Prepare Motion to Terminate Temporary Custody Agreement

Open the dictation file **CS9 MOT-TERMINATE**. Using the court heading information in the respondent's answer, listen and transcribe the motion as a new document. Upon completion, save as **CS9 BELL-MOT-TERMINATE** and print one copy of it.

L E G A L   F O C U S

Discovery in a Divorce Proceeding
The process of discovery in a divorce action is similar to that provided in a civil action, except that the discovery process is focused primarily on obtaining financial data. The emphasis on economics during the discovery process helps enhance the settlement process, which lessens the likelihood of a costly trial or delayed appeal if one party is not satisfied with the outcome. The information gained during discovery will better result in a compromised, "homemade" settlement regarding the division of assets and liabilities between the parties and the financial support for the children. Both parties may then leave the martial relationship with cash settlements or long-term security for themselves or their children in the future.

CS-7 Answer of Respondent

IN THE CIRCUIT COURT OF THE
17TH JUDICIAL CIRCUIT IN AND
FOR BROWARD COUNTY, FLORIDA

CASE NO.: 2X-77925-JL

IN RE: THE MARRIAGE OF

KAREN BELL,

     Petitioner,

and

TROY BELL,

     Respondent.

_____/

RESPONDENT'S ANSWER TO PETITION AND
COUNTERPETITION FORDISSOLUTION OF MARRIAGE

Respondent, TROY BELL, by and his undersigned attorney, responds to the

Petition by Petitioner, KAREN BELL, as follows:

    1. The Respondent admits the allegations contained in paragraphs 1, 2, 3, and 4

of the Petition.

    2. The Respondent denies the allegations contained in paragraphs 8,…

    I HEREBY CERTIFY that a true copy of the foregoing was furnished by mail this

_____ day of_____, 20XX, to Mary Ellen Janetti, Esq., Reginald J.

Davis and Associates, Attorney for Petitioner, 1200 N.E. First Avenue, Suite 500, Fort

Lauderdale, FL 33316-1157.

_____
ROBYN C. WHITNEY, ESQ.
Attorney for Respondent
2112 North Bay Avenue
Davie, FL 33312-2449
Phone: (954) 555-0199
Fax: (954) 555-0112

Prepare Notice of Hearing

Open the file **NOTICE-HEARING** from the Transcription CD. Using the information contained in this document, prepare the notice for the above motion by inserting the required information into the appropriate places in the document. Upon completion, save as **CS10 BELL-NOT-HEARING** and print one copy of it.

Prepare Interim Billing Statement

1. Open the file **BILL-FORM**. Key the client's name and address and current date in the appropriate places on the document.
2. Open the dictation file **CS11 CLIENT BILL**. Listen and transcribe the interim billing dictation by Attorney Janetti. Be sure to add the word "Interim" in the title of the bill. Calculate the final amount due from the client. Upon completion, save as **CS11 BELL-BILL2** and print one copy of the document.

Critical Thinking

What is the advantage and disadvantage for each party being required to submit a financial affidavit during a dissolution of marriage proceeding? Discuss your findings.

Other Divorce Issues

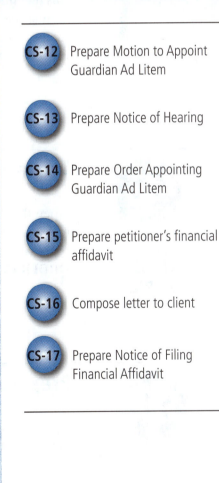

From Attorney Janetti

Because of the ongoing custody problems in this case, I have dictated a motion to appoint a guardian ad litem for the children. Please prepare the motion and set it for a hearing in two weeks before Judge Nixon. I have also dictated a form of an order I will take with me to the hearing. Meanwhile, our client, Karen, has returned a draft copy of her financial affidavit. Please prepare the form in final format. Then compose a letter to Karen, requesting her to come in and sign. Prepare a notice of filing the financial affidavit with the court.

tasks

CS-12 Prepare Motion to Appoint Guardian Ad Litem

CS-13 Prepare Notice of Hearing

CS-14 Prepare Order Appointing Guardian Ad Litem

CS-15 Prepare petitioner's financial affidavit

CS-16 Compose letter to client

CS-17 Prepare Notice of Filing Financial Affidavit

Prepare Motion to Appoint Guardian Ad Litem

Open the dictation file **CS12 AD LITEM MOT**. Using the court heading information for this case, listen to the dictation by Attorney Janetti and transcribe the motion as a new document. Upon completion, save as **CS12 MOTION-GAL** and print one copy of it.

Prepare Notice of Hearing

Open the **NOTICE-HEARING** form. Using the information contained in this document, prepare the notice of hearing for the above motion by inserting the required information into the appropriate places in the document. Upon completion, save as **CS13 BELL-NOT-HEARING2** and print one copy of the notice.

Prepare Order Appointing Guardian Ad Litem

Open the dictation file **CS14 AD LITEM ORDER**. Using the court heading information for this case, listen to the dictation by Attorney Janetti and transcribe the order as a new document. Upon completion, save as **CS-14 ORDER-GAL** and print one copy it.

Prepare Petitioner's Financial Affidavit

Open the file **DOM-FINANCIAL-AFF**. Using the information in the draft of the petitioner's financial affidavit in Figure CS-15, prepare the final form of the affidavit by keying the handwritten figures into the appropriate places on the document. Upon completion, print one copy of the financial affidavit and save as **CS15 BELL-FINANCIAL-AFF**.

CS-15 Affidavit Form with Handwritten Entries

FAMILY LAW FINANCIAL AFFIDAVIT

I, _____Karen LeeAnn Bell_____ , being sworn, certify that the following information is true:

Date of birth:	May 1, 19XX
Occupation:	Bookkeeper
Work address:	Glenn Bros. Const., 790 Industrial Way, N. Miami 33161-2333
Rate of pay (per week):	$500.00 per week salary

SECTION I. PRESENT MONTHLY GROSS INCOME:

Monthly gross salary or wages:	$2,000.00
Monthly bonuses, overtime, or similar payments:	$0
Monthly income from other sources, including disability benefits/SSI, unemployment compensation, pension, alimony (from this case or other cases), interest, dividends, or other sources (list separately):	$0
TOTAL GROSS INCOME:	$2,000.00

PRESENT MONTHLY DEDUCTIONS:

Monthly federal, state, and local income tax:	$300.00		
Filing Status:	Married	Number of Dependents Claimed:	3
Monthly FICA or self-employment taxes:	$ 150.00		
Monthly Medicare payments:	$ 50.00		
Monthly court-ordered child support:	$		
Monthly court-ordered alimony:	$		
Other monthly deductions from pay:	$ 50.00 per month savings		
TOTAL DEDUCTIONS:	$ 250.00		
PRESENT NET MONTHLY INCOME:	$ 1,750.00		

SECTION II. AVERAGE MONTHLY EXPENSES:

A. HOUSEHOLD	
Mortgage or rent	$ 750.00
Property taxes	$ incl.
Utilities	$ 110.00
Telephone	$ 35.00
Food	$ 200.00
Meals outside the home	$ 50.00
Maintenance/repairs	$ 50.00
Other	$

B. AUTOMOBILE	
Car payment	$ 279.00
Gasoline	$ 200.00
Repairs	$ 25.00
Insurance	$ 55.00

C. CHILDREN'S EXPENSES	
Daycare	$ 300.00
Lunch money	$ 80.00
Clothing	$ 25.00
Grooming	$ 20.00

Gifts for holidays	$ 100.00
Medical/dental (uninsured)	$ 50.00
Other:	$

D. INSURANCE	
Medical/dental	$ 118.00
Children's medical/dental	$ 40.00
Life insurance	$ 5.00
Other	$

Bell v. Bell
Financial Affidavit of Karen Bell

Page 1

(continued)

CS-15 Affidavit Form with Handwritten Entries

E. OTHER EXPENSES NOT LISTED ABOVE	
Clothing	$ 35.00
Entertainment	$ 40.00
Gifts	$
Religious org.	$ 75.00
Miscellaneous	$
Other:	$

F. PAYMENTS TO CREDITORS	
Visa	$ 50.00
Palm Department Store	$ 50.00
Great Mart	$ 25.00
	$
	$

TOTAL MONTHLY EXPENSES $ 2,767.00

SUMMARY:	
TOTAL PRESENT MONTHLY NET INCOME	$ 1,750.00
TOTAL MONTHLY EXPENSES:	$ 2,767.00
SURPLUS	$
(DEFICIT)	$ (1,017.00)

SECTION III ASSETS AND LIABILITIES:

ASSETS:	
Cash (on hand)	$ 50.00
Cash (in banks or credit unions)	$ 350.00
Stocks, bonds, and notes	$ 0
Real estate (Home) – half value	$ 120,000.00
Other real estate: Half of vacation home in North Carolina	$ 60,000.00
Automobiles	$ 3,500.00
Other personal property	$ 1,000.00
Retirement plans (Pension, IRA, 401-K, etc.)	$ 0
Other assets	$
	$
	$
	$
	$
	$
Total Assets	$ 184,900.00

LIABILITIES:	
Mortgages on real estate: First mortgage on home– One-half liability	$ 125,000.00
Second mortgage on home – one-half liability	$ 10,000.00
Other mortgages – vacation home, half	$ 20,000.00
Auto loans	$ 8,000.00
Charge/credit card accounts Visa – $ 5,500.00 Palm – $ 2,200.00 Great Mart - $ 1,200.00	$ 8,900.00
Other	$
Total Liabilities	$ 171,900.00

Bell v. Bell
Financial Affidavit of Karen Bell

Page 2

(continued)

CS-15 Affidavit Form with Handwritten Entries

NET WORTH:

Total Assets	$ *184,900.00*
Total Liabilities	$ *171,900.00*
TOTAL NETWORTH	$ *13,000.00*

CONTINGENT ASSETS AND LIABILITIES: If you have any POSSIBLE assets (income potential, bonuses, inheritance) or POSSIBLE liabilities (future unpaid taxes, possible lawsuits, etc.), list them here.

Contingent Assets	
	$
Total Contingent Assets	$

Contingent Liabilities	
Total Contingent Liabilities	$

I understand that I am swearing or affirming under oath to the truthfulness of the claims made in this affidavit and that the punishment for knowingly making a false statement includes fines and/or imprisonment.

Date: _____

_____
Signature of Party

PRINTED NAME: _____

STATE OF FLORIDA

              SS:

COUNTY OF BROWARD

    Sworn to and subscribed before me this _____ day of _____, 20XX.

_____
Notary Public

_____ Personally known
_____ Produced identification
Type of identification produced:
_____

Bell v. Bell
Financial Affidavit of Karen Bell

(concluded)

Compose Letter to Client

When composing a letter to the client, Karen Bell, be sure to inform her that the final form of her financial affidavit is finished and to please make an appointment to come in and sign it. Tell her that when she signs the finalized financial affidavit, it will be notarized in the office and then filed with the court. Finally, tell her that she can call Attorney Janetti if she has any questions about the financial affidavit or the procedure of filing it.

Open the **LETTERHEAD** file. Compose the letter with an envelope to the client with the details indicated. Save as **CS16 BELL-LTR3** and print one copy of the letter and envelope.

Prepare Notice of Filing Financial Affidavit

Open the **DOM-NOTICE-FILING** form. Using the information contained in this document, prepare the pleading by inserting the required information into the appropriate places in the document. Save as **CS17 BELL-NOTICE-FILING** and print one copy of the notice.

L E G A L   F O C U S

Mediation

Divorce mediation, a voluntary process by the parties, is often an effective tool for resolving issues that arise during a divorce action. A mediator, acting as a neutral third party, helps couples identify the issues that need to be resolved and guides them through the decision-making process until a mutually agreeable settlement is reached. Mediation is a less costly and time-consuming process than court litigation, and open communication to achieve common goals is stressed as opposed to finding fault. Issues that can be worked out during mediation include such things as parenting arrangements, support, and the division of assets and debts. Most couples who choose mediation avoid the time-consuming consequences of court litigation and find the process effective in meeting the needs of both parties as they prepare for a new future.

Critical Thinking

Do you believe the appointment of a guardian ad litem should be required for every divorce case where children are involved? Discuss your opinion.

Concluding Documents

From Attorney Janetti

The Bells have come to an agreement regarding the issues of this case. Therefore, prepare the notice of final hearing. Then prepare the marital settlement agreement between the parties that I have dictated as well as a quit claim deed for Troy to sign, giving ownership of the marital home to Karen. Ceylonda has written down the legal description of the property for you to use when preparing these documents. Then prepare the final judgment of dissolution of marriage. Finally, I have dictated a closing letter to Karen along with a final bill in this case for you to prepare.

tasks

CS-18 Prepare Notice of Final Hearing

CS-19 Prepare Marital Settlement Agreement

CS-20 Prepare Quit Claim Deed

CS-21 Prepare Final Judgment of Dissolution of Marriage

CS-22 Prepare letter to client

CS-23 Prepare final billing statement

Prepare Notice of Final Hearing

Open the **NOTICE-HEARING** form. Using the information contained in it, prepare the notice of hearing motion by keying the required information into the appropriate places in the document. Be sure to key the word "FINAL" in the title of this particular hearing notice. Upon completion, save as **CA18 BELL-FINAL-HEARING** and print one copy of the notice.

Prepare Marital Settlement Agreement

Open **DOM-MSA-DRAFT** form. Then open the dictation file **CS19 MARITAL-AGR**. Listen and transcribe the dictation by Attorney Janetti. Insert the legal description provided by Ceylonda in Figure CS-19, in to Section IX of the agreement form. Upon completion, save as **CS19 BELL-MSA** and print one copy of it.

L E G A L   F O C U S

Post-Judgment Issues

Even without an appeal on the judgment, a divorce action is never complete until no further obligations exist between the parties. For example, child support and visitation arrangements may go on for years. During that entire time, the terms of the final judgment or decree are binding on both parties.

Modification proceedings are used to change the terms of the final judgment or decree. One party files a motion, alleging a substantial change of circumstances, either financial or otherwise, and requests relief from the court by changing the final judgment or decree.

All modification proceedings are considered to be a continuation of the original divorce case. The same court heading, case number, and names of the parties are used as in the original dissolution proceeding. The court will hear the matter and make a ruling on the modification, either granting or denying the relief requested.

CS-19 Note from Ceylonda Jones

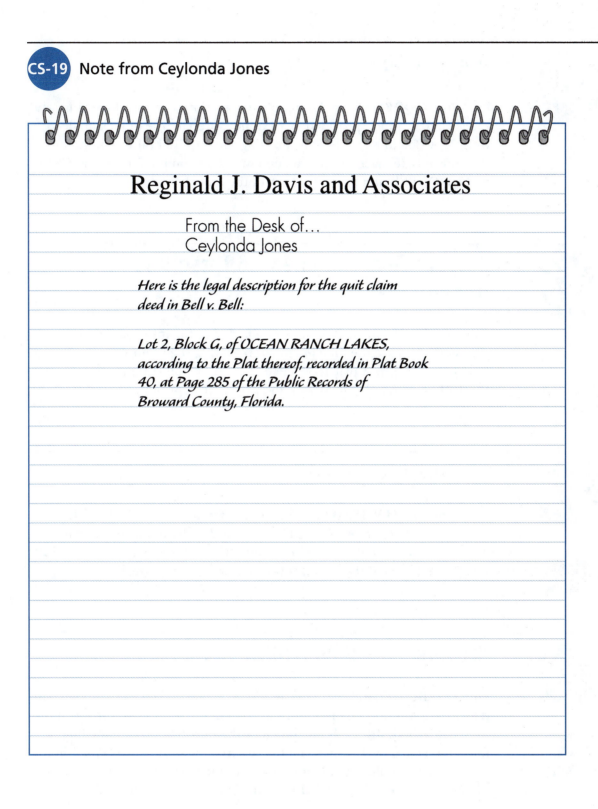

Reginald J. Davis and Associates

From the Desk of...
Ceylonda Jones

*Here is the legal description for the quit claim
deed in Bell v. Bell:*

*Lot 2, Block G, of OCEAN RANCH LAKES,
according to the Plat thereof, recorded in Plat Book
40, at Page 285 of the Public Records of
Broward County, Florida.*

Prepare Quit Claim Deed

Open the **QQDEED** form. Using the information from the document, and the legal description provided by Ceylonda, prepare the quit claim deed from Troy Bell to Karen Bell by inserting the required information in to the appropriate places on the document. Upon completion, save as **CS20 BELL-QQDEED** and print one copy of the quit claim deed.

Prepare Final Judgment of Dissolution of Marriage

Open the **DOM-FINAL-JUDGMENT** file. Using the information in this case study, prepare the final judgment by keying the required information in to the appropriate places on the document. Upon completion, save as **CS21 BELL-FINAL-JUDGMENT** and print one copy of it.

Prepare Letter to Client

Open the **LETTERHEAD** file. Then open the dictation file **CS22 BELL LETTER**. Listen and transcribe the letter and address the envelope to Karen Bell as dictated by Attorney Janetti. Upon completion, save as **CS22 BELL-LTR3** and print one copy of the letter and envelope.

Prepare Final Billing Statement

Open the **BILL-FORM** file. Key the client's name and address and current date in the appropriate places on the document. Then open the dictation file **CS23 FINAL BILL**. Listen and enter the information into the billing form as dictated by Attorney Janetti. Be sure to add the word "Final" in the title of the bill. Calculate the final amount due from the client. Upon completion, save as **CS23 BELL-BILL3** and print one copy of the bill.

Critical Thinking

What are some instances when a party may file a petition for modification of a final divorce decree?

Glossary

Advanced Directive: A legal document that tells others of one's wishes concerning medical care when the person is too sick to make his/her own decisions.

Affidavit: A written statement of facts made under oath before a notary public.

Answer: A pleading filed by the defendant that responds to the complaint by either admitting or denying the claims contained in it.

Articles of Incorporation: The document that officially forms the corporation and states the scope of the business the corporation is authorized to do.

Attorney-in-Fact: The person who is appointed to act for the grantor.

B

Beneficiary: The person named in a will to receive property.

Bill of Sale: A document used to transfer and warrant title to personal property involved in a real estate transaction.

Board of Directors: The body on which the directors serve in order to conduct corporation business.

Bylaws: The rules and regulations adopted by a corporation to govern its ongoing activities.

C

Certificate of Service: A sentence at the end of a pleading in which the attorney attests to the fact that a copy of the pleading was furnished to all the opposing attorneys or parties in the action, set out by name and address.

Closing: The transaction used to complete the agreement made between a seller and a buyer concerning the purchase of real estate.

Complaint: The initial pleading by which a lawsuit is filed with the court.

Conflict of Interest: A situation in which a person (such as an attorney) has a duty to more than one person or organization, but cannot do justice to the actual or potentially adverse interests of both parties.

Corporate Minute Book: A loose-leaf book that contains the recorded proceedings and other papers pertaining to the corporation.

Corporation: An artificial entity created by law for the purpose of conducting a business.

Defendant: The party to whom a claim for damages is directed.

Deposition: A pretrial recorded statement of a party or witness to a lawsuit to determine what that party or witness knows and what that person's testimony will be at trial.

Directors: Representatives elected by the shareholders to conduct the business of the corporation for them.

Discovery: The term used to describe the process by which parties to a lawsuit obtain facts, documents, evidence, and other information about the case in order to prepare for trial.

Duces Tecum: A Latin term meaning "to bring with you," usually used in subpoenas.

Durable Power of Attorney for Health Care: A written document signed by a person giving another person the power to act in making health-care decisions for him/her.

Financial Power of Attorney: A written document signed by a person giving another person the power to act in making financial decisions for him/her.

Formal Will: A will that contains all of the necessary elements required by law to be valid.

Grantee: The person who receives a grant or property.

Grantor: The name given to the person who transfers property.

HIPAA: The Health Insurance Portability and Accountability Act passed by Congress in 2003, which mandates a uniform set of standards to ensure the privacy of an individual's health-care information and to strictly limit unauthorized disclosures without the patient's express permission.

Incorporators: Those who join together to organize a corporation.

Interrogatories: Written questions that are offered by either party to the opposing side, seeking information about a case.

Legal Description: The description by which property is identified according to legal requirements of boundary markings.

Litigation: Any lawsuit or other resort to the courts to determine a legal question or matter.

Living Will: A document outlining how a person wants to be medically treated in the event of a terminal illness or a condition that requires decisions about the use of life-sustaining procedures.

M

Metes and Bounds: A system of describing real property that measures the territorial limits of the property by measuring distance and angles from designated landmarks and in relation to adjoining properties.

Minutes: The recorded proceedings of the corporation.

N

No-Lien Affidavit: An affidavit signed by the seller in a real estate transaction, attesting to the fact that there are no liens or encumbrances on the property being conveyed to the buyer.

Non-Compete Agreement: A contract that states that one person will not compete with his/her employer by engaging in any business of a similar nature as an employee, independent contractor, owner, part owner, significant investor, or other capacity.

Notary Public: A public officer who administers oath, certifies documents, and takes acknowledgments.

Personal Representative: The person (or institution) named by the testator who gathers and distributes the assets of the testator's estate as directed by the will.

Plaintiff: The party who initiates a court action.

Pleadings: Written claims and statements filed with the court during the process of a lawsuit.

Power of Attorney: A legal document in which one person voluntarily gives another person legal authority to act for him/her.

Quiet Title Complaint: A suit filed requesting the court to cancel a claim on real property that could affect ownership of title and to declare a person's ownership in the real estate free and clear.

R

Registered Agent: An individual or domestic corporation who will always be available to accept service of process, on behalf of the corporation, in the event it is sued by another party.

Release: A written document whereby some claim, right, or interest is given up to the person against whom the claim, right, or interest could have been enforced.

Request for Admissions: A written request by one party to the other party requesting that party to admit or deny certain facts, opinions, or applications of law about the case.

Self-Proving Affidavit: A notarized statement added to a will that is later offered for proof that the will was properly signed and that will avoid the necessity of bringing one or more of the witnesses before the court after the testator's death to testify as to the signing of the will.

Shareholders: Individuals who own a share, or portion of a corporation.

Subpoena: A written command issued by the court to appear at a certain time and place in order to give testimony about a case.

Subpoena *Duces Tecum*: A subpoena that is used when the witness is required to bring something to the deposition, such as medical records, reports, or some other evidence in possession of that person. The term *duces tecum* is Latin and means "bring with you."

Summons: An official notification issued by the court to the defendant, giving notice that a complaint has been filed and that a response to the complaint must be made within a specified period of time.

T

Testator: The person making a will.

Voluntary Dismissal: A written cancellation of a lawsuit filed by the plaintiff with the Court.

Warranty Deed: The name given to the deed conveying title in real property from the seller to the buyer, which contains clauses that the seller provides to the buy that act as some protection against claims that might interfere with ownership of the property by the buyer.

Will: A legal document in which a person directs how property is to be distributed after his/her death.